Forward

As you delve into "The Executive Assistant Toolbox" by the ever-dynamic Rita Gunning, prepare to discover a book of invaluable advice and insider knowledge that will fundamentally elevate your professional admin career.

Rita has spent more than three decades mastering the art of being an Executive Assistant. Her experiences are not confined to one place or culture. She's lived in seven countries, offering her services in business hubs like Australia, Hong Kong and Japan. Her exposure to different cultures and work environments has enriched her understanding of the EA role and its universal impact, making this book relevant and useful for a global audience.

Rita's experience extends beyond the Executive Assistant role. She's navigated the challenges of entrepreneurship, running a marketing business in Australia, a café/restaurant in Hollywood, Florida and is a silent partner in a real estate company in Australia. She's been the guiding hand behind successful ventures, understanding the intricate dynamics of business from multiple perspectives. This blend of experiences has provided her with a unique insight into the pressures, expectations, and the rhythm of executive life.

In founding the Executive Assistant Oasis YouTube channel and Facebook group, Rita has created a supportive, thriving community for Executive Assistants to learn, grow, and share experiences globally. Her digital platforms reflect her commitment to empowering others in our profession and are a testament to her passion and dedication.

"The Executive Assistant Toolbox" is the culmination of Rita's professional journey. Inside, you'll find practical tips, in-depth insights, and relatable anecdotes that will guide you through the challenges and victories that define an Executive Assistant's career. Whether you're a junior entering this profession or a seasoned professional, this book is your ticket to becoming a more efficient, resourceful, and confident Executive Assistant.

On a personal note, I couldn't be prouder to write this foreword for Rita's first book. She has been such an amazing support in my admin career professionally and personally as a dear friend. She continues to inspire me with her commitment to assisting admin professionals globally. I'm already looking forward to book #2!

Enjoy this read. It's written with truth and heart.

Sincerely,

Candice Burningham
Career admin of 20+ years, Founder of Admin Avenues, The Executive Support and Director of The Admin Collective.

The Executive Assistant Toolkit

To Josh and Elyse
You Are My Why.

TABLE OF CONTENT

INTRODUCTION -- 2
Once Upon a Time --
PART ONE--- 5
And So It Begins --
PART TWO -- 16
The Set Up Before The Magic Happens! --------------------------------
PART THREE --29
Meetings, Meetings, Meetings! Nobody Got Time for That! ----
PART FOUR ---44
Emails, Invites and Inbox, Oh My! -----------------------------------
PART FIVE ---58
The Daily Grind ---
PART SIX -- 75
Dirty Laundry ---
PART SEVEN--- 85
Checklists Are for Winners --
PART EIGHT --- 100
Tell Me More! ---

INTRODUCTION

Once Upon a Time

Rita Gunning

How I got started

My career path has spanned three decades as an Executive Assistant, a role I never initially envisioned for myself. After leaving school, I embarked on a hairdressing apprenticeship driven by my passion for styling hair. However, the demands of the job took a toll on my health; long hours and no breaks led to anaemia, weight loss, and a realization that hairdressing wasn't my calling.

Uncertain of my next step, I enrolled in a Secretarial College with dreams of becoming a skilled secretary. Back then, proficiency in typing was highly valued, and while I didn't become the fastest typist, I excelled in Shorthand. Sadly, the decline of Shorthand's relevance coincided with the rise of Dictaphones, leaving my Shorthand skills unused.

My first office role involved mundane tasks like typing cheques at a travel company. Despite the monotony, I cherished working there due to the perk of a free world tour. Within just nine months, I was promoted from typist to assistant of an Executive Assistant. This marked the beginning of my journey in the executive realm, and I was merely 19 at the time. The executive assistant I worked under imparted valuable knowledge, setting the stage for my career as an Executive Assistant.

Since that pivotal experience, I've traversed through numerous industries, working for a plethora of titles including CEOs, Directors, Managing Directors, and more. The knowledge I've amassed from each executive, whether positive or challenging, has been invaluable.

My husband's work-related relocations led me to different countries, where my executive assistant skills opened doors to new job opportunities. My professional ventures have spanned Australia, Japan, Hong Kong, and the US. While offers came in from Dubai, Saudi Arabia, and the UK, I declined them due to various reasons.

The Executive Assistant Toolkit

In the midst of my 30-year journey as an executive assistant, I juggled motherhood, owned an Australian-based Virtual Assistant / Marketing company, silently partnered with an Australian Real Estate firm, and even ventured into the hospitality industry with a restaurant/café in Hollywood, Florida.

I've also taken my expertise online as the founder of the YouTube channel "Executive Assistant Oasis," along with a private Facebook Group under the same name. Despite my varied endeavours, I've consistently circled back to my true passion: the role of an executive assistant.

My commitment to self-improvement remains unwavering. Every year, I dedicate myself to learning something new that enhances my skills. I devour educational content on YouTube, acquire certifications through LinkedIn, and devour books that expand my knowledge.

This longevity and success can be attributed to my openness to challenges and unrelenting desire to learn. Embracing these principles has allowed me to thrive in my role and create a meaningful, enduring career.

Rita Gunning

PART ONE

And So It Begins

Fifteen Things to Do in Your First Ninety Days as an Executive Assistant

The first few weeks of starting a new job are bound to be filled with uncertainty and doubt, having a plan is the key to help you transition into the role smoothly. Here is a transition plan that has worked well for me, broken down in three stages, thirty, sixty and ninety days.

Within the first thirty days:
- Sit down with your executive and discuss their schedule. Find out what their average day looks like and what their biggest priority is. Discuss what objectives your executive needs you to achieve during probation.
- Find out if your executive is a morning or afternoon person. If they are a morning person, they may prefer to work on projects in the morning or reply to emails at that time and prefer all their meetings in the afternoon.
- Review any handover notes you were given when you started and apply the instructions when required.
- Complete the required onboarding training and read up on any policies and procedures that may affect your role.
- Find out if there are any meetings you need to attend, both internally and externally.
- Find out what has and hasn't worked for your executive with their former executive assistants. Make sure you take notes.
- Find an organizational chart and review it; get to know who's who, especially who your executive's direct reports are.
- Set up meetings for yourself with your executive's direct reports individually and get to know them. Find out what they do. Ask them what their experience is working with your executive.
- Set up meetings for yourself with other executive assistants in the company and get to know them and gain insight about how the company runs. Find out more information about your executive and other helpful tips.

- If you have access to your executive's mailbox, make sure you read everything that comes in and everything your executive sends out. You will gain a wealth of knowledge doing this.

Within thirty to sixty days:
- Check in with your executive to find out how you are tracking from their point of view and discuss what is and isn't working, then find a solution and tweak the process.
- Find out more about the company; who the competitors and who the strategic partners are.
- Meet up with the executive assistants again and raise any questions you may have; make sure you are not breaching confidentiality.
- Review and adjust the notes you made in your first thirty days; they will probably need to be updated.

Within sixty to ninety days:
- Review and collate the handover notes and all the notes you've made over the last ninety days and make any changes. What is the constant that happens every month? You now have enough information to create a process and procedure manual.
- The process and procedure manual will continue to evolve as you continue to evolve within the company.
- Now that you have reached your three months, sit down with your executive to discuss the objectives that were set when you started and how they were achieved. Give your feedback about your ninety-day journey and get their feedback.

Business Acumen for Executive Assistants

Executive Assistants are allrounders, and for you to be successful in your role, you require strong business acumen. So, what is business acumen? Business acumen is the ability to combine your knowledge, your experiences, and your perspective into making decisions. It's about knowing how the business you work in operates.

If an executive assistant understands the business, it helps them assist their executive at a much higher level. They become part of the organisation and team rather than someone who works separately from everyone else.

Let me ask you three questions:
1. Do you know how your company makes money?
2. Would you be able to give a company tour and explain the roles of each department?
3. Do you know what creates growth for your company?

If you are able to answer yes to these three questions, then you are doing well.

An executive assistant is the eyes and ears of the executives and the team. They help connect the dots between departments and team members. They keep the communication and information flowing and the projects moving forward; they also hold things together.

I will point out a few of the tasks an executive assistant is asked to perform; however, the list is much longer. An executive assistant may be asked to:
- Produce reports and presentations.
- Maintain databases.
- Manage projects.
- Organize events.
- Organize travel.
- Diary management.
- Draft, transcribe, edit, and proofread documents.
- Prepare financial statements and the list goes on.

Some of the hats the executive assistant wears:
- Marketer
- Leader
- Entrepreneur
- Negotiator
- Event planner
- Travel agent
- Project manager and much more

To develop business acumen, it's important that an executive assistant asks questions and does additional research when they don't understand something.

Some other ways to develop business acumen:
- Read about business operations.
- Subscribe to professional or industry-associated newsletters.
- Enrol in courses, either online or your local community college; your workplace may even pay for these courses when you graduate.
- Participate in company projects or committees; this will give you a deeper understanding of how your company runs.
- Ask if you can job shadow or sit with a different team or department for a few hours each month to learn what they do at a deeper level.
- Join an executive assistant group where you are able to ask questions and share your knowledge with each other.

Once you start to understand how your organisation makes money, you will begin to know how your business fits into the overall industry and the bigger picture, and your input will become more valuable.

There is a lot of confusion regarding the difference between the personal assistant, the executive assistant, the administrative assistant, and the chief of staff, so I'll shed some light on this topic.

Personal Assistant vs. Executive Assistant

These two titles are used interchangeably, but there are differences in the roles. A personal assistant mainly reports to an individual, such as a celebrity or an athlete or someone outside the corporate world. They not only take care of their boss but also the needs of the family. The personal assistant runs their employer's day-to-day errands and might even travel with them. The tasks of the personal assistant affect their employer directly. Whereas the executive assistant reports to an executive of a company.

The executive assistant, although they report directly to their executive, their actions affect the company as a whole. The personal assistant is embedded in the employer's life, while an executive assistant is embedded in the executive's job.

Difference Between the Executive Assistant vs Administrative Assistant

In the hierarchy of business, the executive assistant would be a higher-level position than an administrative assistant, but both jobs are valuable to a business. Administrative assistants are typically in charge of running the office and taking care of basic clerical duties.

They generally provide operational/administrative tasks to a department, or a specific business function, even if they report to an executive of a company.

Some of the tasks include, but not limited to:
- scheduling and calendar management
- meeting preparation and travel planning
- organizing and managing paperwork
- data entry and reporting
- drafting and proofreading communications

- fielding inquiries from clients and other business associates
- creating and improving operational processes and procedures

Executive assistants generally provide support to a single high-level individual or a small group of high-level people, such as a CEO, presidents, and vice presidents of companies. Executive Assistants are trusted to handle things that are more sensitive and private to the business, so discretion and good judgment are essential skills.

In most cases, the executive assistant handles some of the same tasks as administrative assistants; they are also expected to manage more, including but not limited to:
- overseeing projects and critical tasks
- planning office design and layout improvements
- anticipating needs and ensuring the executive is prepared for anything
- offering advice and guidance with regards to prioritizing and managing deadlines
- problem solving before issues reach the executive's desk
- planning events
- coordinating travel
- acting as an alter ego, attending meetings, or responding to emails on behalf of the executive
- creating presentations and reports, and
- researching

The best executive assistants act as partners with the executives they support. They must understand not only the intricate details of the executive's job, but also how they think and make decisions.

To sum it up, both the executive and the administrative assistant offer advanced administrative support for managers and executives. What separates their roles is that the administrative assistant's role is more routine and focused on operational and clerical tasks for a team or department. The executive assistant's role has a level of confidentiality and responsibility and focuses on partnering up with a top-level executive.

Difference between Chief of Staff vs. Executive Assistant

The executive assistant and the chief of staff roles are intertwined, and some executive assistants will read the following and think, *I already do all this.* I too have performed the role of a chief of staff but under the title of an executive assistant.

Employees generally look for chief of staff candidates with a minimum of a bachelor's degree in a relevant field, such as:
- public administration
- business administration

The chief of staff role is considered the next step up from being an executive assistant. These are some of the differences between the chief of staff and an executive assistant:
- They typically serve as a strategic advisor and has a more active role in the overall management of an organization, while an executive assistant is more focused on administrative tasks and providing support to the executive.
- They typically work closely with the executive to manage their calendar and provide strategic advice, while an executive assistance role is more focused on day-to-day tasks such as scheduling meetings, taking notes, and managing communications.
- They may have a higher level of authority and responsibility than an executive assistant.
- They may be responsible for developing and executing strategies to help the executive reach their goals, while an executive assistant's primary role is to provide administrative support to the executive.
- They may have a larger team to manage and oversee, while an executive assistant may only work with a small team.
- They may have a larger budget to manage and allocate, while an executive assistance budget is normally allocated to them.

- They are usually involved in the planning and budgeting of finances, whereas an executive assistant will be given a budget to work with.
- They are typically more involved in the long-term planning and vision of the organization, while an executive assistant is more focused on the day-to-day operations.
- They may manage projects for company-wide initiatives, whereas an executive assistant may manage projects but on a much smaller scale.
- They are seen as the top advisor and closest confidant to the executive, whereas an executive assistant is often seen as a right-hand person to the executive.

How to Build Trust with Your Executive

Executive assistants work closely with their executives, so it is imperative to develop a good relationship. If you don't have that, it will put you at a disadvantage and will affect your work. In the years I have been an executive assistant, I have used the following techniques I consider essential in developing harmony, trust, and respect from my executive.

Building rapport: Organize a time with your executive each day, preferably morning, to discuss if there is anything they need you to do that day. It is also a time to discuss what is on your to-do list and what was achieved the day before.

When you first start at a company, ask these work-related questions:
- Is your executive a morning or afternoon person?
- Would they prefer to work on projects they need to focus on in the morning or afternoon?

Break the ice and ask personal questions, such as:
- Did they have a nice weekend?

- If they play a sport in the evening or weekends, ask them how it went.
- Questions relating to their family (not too personal), anything they have talked to you about prior.

This helps build rapport, and you might find you have something in common. Listen to what they say in conversations with you or others; they might mention their likes and dislikes that you can take note of.

Build business acumen: Understand what the business does and what each department is responsible for. Ask if you can attend some meetings with your executive. The more you know about the business, the more you can help your executive.

Offer your assistance: If your executive is working on a project, ask them if there are certain parts of that project you can help with. Show initiative, don't wait to be asked to assist. If they take you up on your offer, then overdeliver. This will demonstrate to your executive that you are proactive.

Show them you have their back: If your executive is really busy and may have forgotten to complete a task, give them a gentle prompt and add that task to their calendar and mark it as a 'to-do' item. Prove to them that you can sort out matters in their absence, and at the next catchup, let them know what transpired and how you resolved it. Always ask if they were okay with the decision you made. This will show them you are trying to make decisions you think they would approve of.

Use your initiative: Don't wait to be told what to do and don't ask your executive how to do things unless it is something only they would know. Work things out for yourself; do your research. It's amazing what you can find on YouTube or when you do a Google search.

Own your job: Your job is yours; you can grow it by looking at ways you can help the business. It might be researching prices of stationery and negotiating with suppliers for the best deals. It could be a process you think can be simplified; do the research and document it.

Keep learning: There is so much you can learn on the internet that can make your work life easier. There are many tips and tricks on Outlook, Word, Excel, and other software you use that will make a process go smoothly.

Be early: Be at least fifteen minutes early; it will show your executive they can rely on you to be in on time. It will also help you get on top of things when you get in to work, so by the time you are meant to start, you are prepared. An executive assistant should always prepare for their tomorrow before they leave work the day before.

Be accountable: Take responsibility for any mistakes you make. This will help build trust with your executive. Don't try to put blame on others. We all make mistakes, and owning up to a mistake will show your executive you are honest, so when something happens and it's not your fault, you will be believed.

Have a sense of humour: I cannot stress this enough. In the life of an executive assistant, the day can get crazy and frustrating, but it makes the job easier when you can laugh at things and just accept that this craziness is all part of the role.

PART TWO

The Set Up Before The Magic Happens!

The Importance of Creating an Executive Assistant Manual

In each new role I've undertaken, if I'm lucky, I've received a handful of sheets comprising of handover notes, serving as a reference point for the transition. However, when departing from a position, I've consistently left behind an Executive Assistant Manual – a comprehensive resource spanning a minimum of 50 pages. This manual encompasses a cover page and a meticulously organized table of contents, all tailored for seamless navigation.

The concept of functioning without such a manual as an executive assistant seems almost implausible to me, particularly during the initial year. This time frame is when the memory of sporadic tasks might begin to fade, leaving one in a situation where a task needs completing, but the method remains elusive. This is where the true value of an executive assistant manual shines – it's a beacon of efficiency. The manual empowers an assistant to excel by eradicating the need for incessant inquiries about processes already familiar but momentarily obscured.

Reflecting on my role as an executive assistant to a CEO, I'm inclined to share a glimpse of the contents of my own manual. Naturally, your manual will be uniquely crafted to match your responsibilities. Think of this as an illustrative example – a starting point. Just as my manual continues to evolve in tandem with my role's growth, so too will yours.

Table of Contents
Executive Assistant Position Description --- 3
Executive Assistant KPI -- 4
Executive Assistant Typical Day -- 5
CEO Travel & Misc Information -- 7
    Travel Club Information -- 7
    Passport & Licence Details -- 7
    Credit Cards -- 7

The Executive Assistant Toolkit

- Car Registration --------- 7
- CEO's Leave Request --------- 7
- Leadership Team Travel --------- 7
- Business Travel --------- 7
- CEO Misc Information --------- 7
- Sydney Preferred Restaurants --------- 8
- Sydney Cafes --------- 8
- Melbourne Restaurant Ideas --------- 8
- Office Information --------- 9
  - Boardroom Air Con Repair --------- 9
  - Catering --------- 9
  - Cleaner --------- 9
  - Courier --------- 9
  - Document Bin --------- 9
  - IT Issues --------- 9
  - Mail Box --------- 9
  - Maintenance --------- 9
  - Office Pass Register --------- 9
  - Property Manager Details --------- 9
  - Security Details --------- 9
  - Stationery --------- 9
  - Testing & Tagging --------- 10
  - Water Dispenser --------- 10
  - Building Business Lounge --------- 10
- Office Address (Australia / International) --------- 11
- Industry Executives and their Executive Assistants List --------- 12
  - 2023 Christmas Card (Clients/Staff) --------- 14
  - 2024 Christmas Card (Clients/Staff) --------- 14
- Executive Assistant List and Their Executives --------- 15
- Meeting Information --------- 18
  - Board Meeting Agenda Sample --------- 18
  - Board Members --------- 20
  - Risk Committee Meeting & Members --------- 20
- 2023 Meetings Schedules --------- 21

Rita Gunning

- Board Meeting & Risk Committee Meetings – 2023 — 21
- All Staff Quarterly Town Hall Meetings — 21
- Monthly Leadership Team Meeting 2023 — 21
- Performance Reviews & Calibration Meeting Schedule — 22
- Leadership Team 1:1 Meeting with CEO — 22
- Sample Email to be Sent to LT Team Before Scheduling 1:1 for the Year — 23
- Offsite – All Staff Conference Details — 23
- Leadership Team Details & End of Year Holiday Roster and Delegation List — 25
  - Leadership Team Birthdays and Birthday Notification Approval — 25
  - Chairman 1:1 Catchup with CEO — 25
  - Leadership Team (LT) Members Details — 25
  - State Sales Managers Details — 25
  - End of Year – Leadership Team Christmas Leave — 26
  - End of Year Delegation Plan — 26
- Client Quarterly Meetings 2023 — 27
- System & Software Instructions — 28
  - ESS (Employee Self Service) — 28
  - Elmo — 30
  - Compliance Modules — 31
  - Zoom Webinar Instructions — 32
  - Zoom Delegated Outlook Procedure — 32
  - Zoom Presentation Camera Size/Scale Change — 32
  - Jira Tickets — 33
  - Concur (Expense Reconciliation) — 34
  - Trivia Events — 37
  - Golf Charity Days — 37
  - Uploading on SharePoint — 38
- Misc Checklist and Annual To-Do List — 40
  - Travel Itinerary Template — 43
  - End of Year Checklist – In October — 45
  - Travel Checklist — 47
  - Annual Things To-Do List by Month Checklist — 49

We know how hard it is for an executive assistant to start a new job, so when I leave, I try and leave the place for the next executive assistant better than when I started... I hope you do too.

The Importance of Having an Executive Assistant's List

Within my executive assistant manual, I maintain a roster of executive assistants associated with the executives my CEO engages with or has previously interacted with.

If you are working in a new company and your executive asks you to contact an external executive, you won't know who their executive assistant is unless your executive tells you the name and gives you the details.

When engaging directly with an executive via email, my approach involves introducing myself within the email's preamble. Following this introduction, I transcribe the message as directed by my executive. In the same communication, I take the liberty to inquire about the presence of an executive assistant. If one is indeed in the picture, I politely request the addition of their contact details in the subsequent correspondence. This seamless inclusion allows me to establish a channel of communication with them moving forward. Once I receive a response, I integrate the executive assistant's information into the list alongside the executive's name. At times, direct feedback might not materialize from the executive, but instead, a response is received from their executive assistant.

Rita Gunning

Here is what the list looks like:

Contact	Email address	EA contact details	Office location
Adrian Robson ☆	Adrian@emailaddress.com	Camilla Marshal Camilla@emailaddress.com Mobile XXX XXX XXX	Executive Job Title Address Executive Mobile XXX XXX XXX
Allan Cooper	allan@emailaddress.com	Jasmin Reynolds jasmin@emailaddress.com Mobile XXX XXX XXX	Executive Job Title Address Executive Mobile XXX XXX XXX
Andrew Winterstein ☆	andrew@emailaddress.com	Megan Segeil megan@emailaddress.com	Executive Job Title Address Executive Mobile XXX XXX XXX
Andrew Fraser ☆	Andrew@emailaddress.com	Sarah Correll sarah@emailaddress.com.au Mobile XXX XXX XXX	Executive Job Title Address Executive Mobile XXX XXX XXX
Andrew Godden	andrew.godden@bmsgroup.com		Executive Job Title Address Executive Mobile XXX XXX XXX
Ben Burcher	benb@emailaddress.com	Channen Ramsey channen@emailaddress.com Mobile XXX XXX XXX	Executive Job Title Address Executive Mobile XXX XXX XXX
Benjamin Button ☆	Ben@emailaddress.com		Executive Job Title Address Executive Mobile XXX XXX XXX
Brendan Roger ☆	broger@emailaddress.com		Executive Job Title Address Executive Mobile XXX XXX XXX
Bruce Bridges	Bridges@emailaddress.com		Executive Job Title Address Executive Mobile XXX XXX XXX
Carl Sutton	carl@emailaddress.com		Executive Job Title Address Executive Mobile XXX XXX XXX
Chris Michaels ☆	Chris@emailaddress.com	Michelle Lyons/Jennifer michelle@emailaddress.com Mobile XXX XXX XXX	Executive Job Title Address Executive Mobile XXX XXX XXX
Christopher Shiloh ☆	Christopher@emailaddress.com	Annette Mocha Annette@emailaddress.com Mobile XXX XXX XXX	Executive Job Title Address Executive Mobile XXX XXX XXX
Craig Robinson ☆	crobinson@emailaddress.com		Executive Job Title Address Executive Mobile XXX XXX XXX

- The list is in alphabetical order by the first name of the executive.
- Next column, I add the executive's email address.
- Next column, I add the executive assistant's name, and under their name, I add their email address and then the mobile number.
- In the last column, I add the executive's job title, address, and phone number.

It honestly doesn't matter how you set your list up, the key lies in its coherence and effectiveness within your context. The objective is to devise a system that resonates with you, one that you comprehend effortlessly and can readily turn to for guidance.

If you're employed within a sizable multinational corporation, it's wise to fashion a similar list for the executive assistants you engage with within your own company, along with the executives they support. This practice proves particularly advantageous, especially during the initial stages of assuming your new role.

Within my list, certain executives are marked with a star, while others remain unmarked. The individuals distinguished by these stars are recipients of a Christmas e-card courtesy of my executive. As October approaches, I review the list in collaboration with my CEO, adding additional stars next to new names introduced over the year. Conversely, there is a possibility of retraction for executives who were extended Christmas e-cards in the preceding year.

Instead of having different lists, you could use this list and add different symbols that denote different tasks you need to perform. In this example, I only show the stars, but in my manual, I also have a different symbol besides the names of the executives my CEO needs to meet up with once a quarter and a different symbol for monthly meetings. This reduces the lists I create for different functions and allows me to work more efficiently.

Executive or Administrative Assistant – Your Passport to Any Industry

Were you aware that the skills you cultivate as an executive assistant serve as a versatile passport to any industry you aspire to enter? Possessing adeptness as an executive assistant opens doors to the industry of your choosing, granted you apply for the role and ace the interview.

At times, you might find the need to enhance your skill set before pursuing positions in a particular sector. For instance, envision a desire to enter the medical field; in this scenario, enrolling in a concise medical administration course could earn you a vital certification – yes, such courses do exist.

Likewise, if your ambition is to join the legal realm, a legal administration course can prove advantageous in propelling you into this domain. However, lack of these certifications shouldn't deter you from applying; don't hesitate to submit your application. You might discover an employer willing to take you on, allowing you to accumulate new skills on the job.

I'm a true believer in going for things you may think you will never get, even if you only meet 60% of the criteria. If you don't try, the answer will always be no; if you do try, the answer may be yes. You may win the interviewer over. I will touch on the 60% rule a little later.

For those harbouring aspirations to transition from one industry to another, the role of an executive assistant serves as an invaluable gateway. Initiate your journey by securing this position, and subsequently, seize the chance to apply for your desired roles within the same company. Should your intent to pivot be sincere, then enrol and complete external courses aligned with your desired field. Communicate this endeavour to your employer; there's a chance they might even reimburse you for your course upon completion.

My tenure as an executive assistant has not only facilitated employment during my global travels – within the confines of proper visas, of course – but has also allowed me to operate in a diverse array of countries. While some countries didn't allow me to work due to visa constraints, other regions, acknowledging my executive assistant background, were inclined to sponsor me.

Let me share the countries and industries in which I've applied my skills as an executive assistant. One of these countries,

Japan, isn't predominantly English-speaking; nevertheless, international firms are open to hiring individuals like you.
Australia:
Travel; Private school; Hospitality; Events; Technology; Real estate; Finance; Insurance; Start-ups

Japan:
Private international school

Hong Kong:
International law firm; Private international school

USA:
Property development company; Hospitality

Beyond my work in these countries, I've encountered opportunities to assume executive assistant roles in Dubai, Saudi Arabia, and the UK, although I declined those positions for various reasons. I share this not to boast, but to highlight the possibilities available. If opportunities come your way, do thorough research and take the plunge. If you don't try, you will never know what is possible.

Whatever you set out to do – find a way to do it!

Applying for a Job with 60% Experience

Have you ever come across a job opening that piqued your interest, yet hesitated to apply because you didn't align perfectly with every single criterion outlined in the description? If you have, you're certainly not alone – a Harvard Study conducted by Tara Sophia Mohr in 2014 revealed that this reservation affects 40% of individuals.

If you find yourself within that 40%, I'm here to convey a crucial message: you don't need to fulfill every single item on the checklist to secure the position. In fact, possessing just 60% of the qualities specified in the job description warrants a bold application. Allow me to elaborate on the rationale behind this perspective:

The stipulations outlined in a job description signify the employer's preferences rather than strict prerequisites; they remain open to candidates who fulfill at least 60% of the listed criteria. What takes precedence for them is finding the ideal fit for the role, and this includes factoring in an individual's personality and demeanour.

Above all else, a well-crafted résumé is paramount to securing your initial foothold. Ensure its clarity by avoiding clutter and incorporating a brief summary statement.

Wondering what a summary statement entails? It's a concise overview designed to capture the employer's attention by spotlighting your qualifications. Recognize that an employer might not peruse your entire résumé, so a summary offers a snapshot of your professional journey, accomplishments, and proficiencies. Strive to maintain its concision; a paragraph or two should be adequate. While the summary statement can be a comprehensive sentence, the rest of your résumé ought to be presented in bullet points.

Subsequently, the next pivotal step involves acing your interview. This crucial interaction significantly enhances your prospects of landing the position.

Interviewing for that Job!

Despite accumulating over three decades of experience as an executive assistant, collaborating with high-ranking executives, I still encounter aspects within job descriptions that are entirely novel to me. Allow me to offer an example: a company might employ software tools I've never had exposure to. Yet, such disparities won't deter me from applying.

When faced with an interview opportunity, I do preliminary preparations the day prior to the interview, not only about the company I am interviewing for, but I go on to YouTube to find out about the software that I am unfamiliar with. If I am asked in an interview whether I have used the software, I always tell the truth, but I also mention I have done a lot of research on the software and understand the concept of what it's used for and how it's used, and I know I won't have a problem learning it.

Being nervous before an interview is natural; however, you can do some things to help relieve or reduce that nervousness. What helps me prepare for my interview is, telling myself it doesn't matter if I get this job or not; it's good experience that will help me get better at interviews. I am going in there, I am going to be confident and am going to be myself.

I tell myself: the interviewers are not better than me! They also had to go through the interview process to get their jobs this company would be lucky to have me as one of their employees.

The reason I do this is because it shifts my mindset, gives me confidence, and helps me believe in myself, my skills, and my value. I have gone through this mindset shift so many times. I am now confident in my skills and my value. If you come across confident in an interview, you set the stage and change the mindset of those around you.

The same kind of positive self-talk and self-assurance that can bolster your confidence in interviews can also be employed when negotiating your desired salary. Reminding yourself of your worth and the reasons you deserve the compensation you're requesting can be a powerful tool.

For instance, you might reiterate to yourself: "I've consistently invested in honing my skills and keeping myself updated. I've dedicated effort to my education, propelling me to the position

I occupy today. I'm not just qualified for this role; I genuinely merit the remuneration I'm seeking."

Even before you step into the interview room, it's crucial to establish a clear figure for your desired salary. Do your online research, aiming for the upper range and even adding a 10% buffer. This is a strategic move, as many companies might aim to negotiate the figure downward during discussions. By setting your initial ask higher, you provide yourself with a bit of negotiation room without jeopardizing your desired outcome.

This salary question can come up at your very first interview; it's happened to me several times. I am happy when they mention the salary in the first interview because I want them to know right from the start what salary I expect. I don't want to waste my time going to second and third interviews, then turning down the job because they can't afford my expertise.

When confronted with the sensitive topic of your current salary during an interview, it's perfectly acceptable to politely decline to disclose that information. A tactful way to respond to this inquiry is to say: "I prefer to keep my current salary private. However, my salary expectation for this role is [mention your expected salary]. I've done thorough research, and I believe this amount aligns with the market rate for someone possessing my skillset."

Crucially, stand firm on your salary expectation and refrain from lowering it due to not meeting 100% of the job criteria. It's worth emphasizing that reaching 100% proficiency in the role is a plausible trajectory within a short span, typically around three months. Once you've acclimated to the role and achieved full competence, renegotiating your salary upward might prove challenging. Thus, it's prudent to ensure your initial compensation aligns with your perceived value and the market standard.

I once had a managing director give me more than I expected as a salary; he increased my salary before I started my first day because of the experience I had, and I didn't meet 100% of the job description. This has only happened once in my career. Working with this executive showed me that he knew the value of good employees.

Engaging in consistent positive self-talk can indeed reshape your mindset over time, empowering you to approach interviews with an inherent confidence. It's important to remember that not securing a particular job should not be perceived as a personal failure. Rejections are a part of the journey, a shared experience even for candidates who fulfill 100% of the criteria. This should never discourage you; your moment will arrive.

A crucial point to bear in mind, especially when navigating a situation where you fulfill 60% of the criteria, is the significance of direct application to the company. When relying on recruiters, your profile might be evaluated alongside other executive assistants in their database, potentially resulting in a missed opportunity. Opting for a direct application to the company enables you to showcase your unique qualifications and attributes, increasing your chances of securing an interview. Once you've earned that opportunity, it's in your hands to make a lasting impression and secure the role.

PART THREE

Meetings, Meetings, Meetings! Nobody Got Time for That!

How to Create a Minutes Template.

Constructing a minute template and drafting meeting Minutes need not be as intimidating as it might appear. Here are some valuable insights. To be honest, taking Minutes is my least favourite task. It's important to understand that there's no universal approach to Minute-taking. Each organization has its own preferences for how Minutes should be crafted. For newcomers, observing past agendas and Minutes can offer valuable guidance on the established style.

Before entering a meeting, ensure your template is primed and that you're well-prepared. Let's delve into what elements should be encompassed within your minute template:

- **Logo:** While not obligatory, some companies prefer having their logo on the template for branding.
- **Company Name and Title:** Include the company's name and the designation "Minutes & Action Points."
- **Meeting Description:** Clearly state the purpose of the meeting, like the "Executive Team's Monthly Meeting" in the example I provided.
- **Date and Time:** Note down the precise date and starting time of the meeting.
- **Meeting Location:** Specify where the meeting is taking place.
- **Meeting Opened:** Record the time at which the meeting officially commenced.
- **Attendees:** List the names of individuals present at the meeting.
- **Absentees:** Note the names of those who were expected but couldn't attend.
- **Additional Attendees:** Highlight any guest speakers or other individuals who joined the meeting.
- **Action Points:** Dedicate space to capture the action items arising from the meeting discussions.

An important step is to align your template with the agenda. Ensure all agenda items are mirrored within the Minutes template.

Remember, while these are the core components, your organization's preferences may prompt variations. With this template foundation, you'll be well-equipped to seamlessly create accurate and informative meeting Minutes.

AGENDA

Meeting	EAO Executive Team Monthly Meeting
Date	Wednesday 9th February 2022
Time	9:00am – 10:30am
Location	Boardroom, 1 Bonnie Street, Richmond
Chair	Wendy Smith
Invitees	Leadership Team

	Agenda Item	Time	Who
1	CEO Welcome & Update	5 mins	WS
2	IQ Scorecard (to be circulated prior and will be assume as read) Discussion to focus on: • Key wins • Misses, reasons, actions, responsibilities	20 mins	All
3	P&L Review Month, YTD and forecast (if applicable)	10 mins	NU
4	Strategy Check In • Platform • Customer • People	10 mins	Platform: TK Customer: DN People: BB
5	Around the grounds Each LT to discuss: • Key focus area next month • Biggest challenge (if any)	25 mins	All
6	People & Culture • Staff movements & vacancies • COVID	5 mins	BB
7	AOB • Who will be our guest speaker at the next meeting?	10 min	All

```
                    EAO MINUTES & ACTION POINTS
                    EXECUTIVE TEAM MONTHLY MEETING
Meeting Date – 9th February 2022
Time: 9:00am – 10:30am
Location: Held in Boardroom of 1 Bonnie Street, Richmond NSW 2753
Meeting Opened – 9:00am

Attendees
    Wendy Smith (Chair)      Danny Nolan        Terry King
    Nathan Union             Ben Burrows        Rachel Grover

Absentees

Others

Action Points
19 January 2022
| Item | Description                                                  | LT Member | Due Date |
| 1    | Write a report to reflect our losses against the wins from 2021 | SA & TK   | Apr 2022 |

                        1. CEO Welcome & Update
  •
                        2. Scorecard
  •
                        2. P&L Review
  •
                        4. Strategic Check-In
  •
                        5. Around the Grounds
  •
                        6. People & Culture
  •
                        Any Other Business
  •

Meeting ended: 10:10 am
Next Meeting: Wednesday 30th March 2022

Signed as correct record
Date: ...........
Signed: ...........
Name (print): ...........
```

On the agenda, number 1 is 'CEO Welcome and Update,' and on my Minute template, the number 1 item is 'CEO Welcome & Update.'

Number 2 on the agenda is the score card, and on my Minute template, it's the same.

Concluding the minutes effectively encompasses a few key details. These elements bring closure to the document and provide a comprehensive record of the meeting's proceedings:

- **Meeting End Time:** Note the time at which the meeting concluded.
- **Date of Next Meeting:** If the next meeting has already been scheduled, include the date of that meeting for reference.
- **Signature Section:** While not obligatory for most meetings, consider adding a dedicated area for signatures. This becomes particularly pertinent for board meetings that could undergo auditing. Notably, the signature should only be appended to the final version of the minutes.

By integrating these concluding elements, your minutes document becomes a well-rounded record of the meeting, capturing its inception, proceedings, and eventual closure.

How to Write Minutes

In the 'Welcome & Update' section, the Minutes are discussed and approved and any outstanding action points are brought up; if they have been completed, they get taken off the next Minutes.

You don't need to capture every word spoken in meetings; you need to have enough information that if someone missed a meeting, they would have an idea of what was discussed. Minutes are also a recap for everyone who attended the meeting.

So this is the recommended course of action.
- With your template ready to go, take your Minutes in real time. The meeting should follow the agenda.
- Be concise and don't capture every word.
- Stick to facts and not someone's theory.
- Don't add any derogatory comments.

- Once the meeting has concluded, add the time the meeting ended.
- If you missed parts of what someone said, send them an email straight after the meeting and ask them to fill in the blanks and return to you by the end of the day. That way, what they said is still on their mind.
- Any action points discussed in the current meeting need to be added to the new Minutes.

Once you get the blank sections completed, you send the draft Minutes to the person in charge, which may be the chair or the facilitator of the meeting, and ask them to review the Minutes before you send them to the attendees and absentees. It's best to send the Minutes within the first few days after the meeting.

A draft agenda is to be sent out a week before the next meeting to see if anyone wants to add any items to the 'Any Other Business' section, also known as the acronym AOB. Give them a day and a half to respond, add any additions to the agenda, and send out the final version of the agenda three days before the next meeting.

Meeting Management Tips

I'm sure you have been stuck in meetings that seem pointless and you walk out with no clear direction on what to do next. It's frustrating. The reality is meetings can have good outcomes, but they take a bit of preparation beforehand. Meetings are meant to boost productivity and efficiency. When everyone is on the same page and aware of what should be done, even the most challenging tasks can be completed.

Love them or hate them, you can't completely eliminate meetings. It's important to make them as useful and constructive as possible. So, without wasting anymore time, let's go over meeting management tips for higher productivity!

Before scheduling a meeting, ask the following questions:
- Is the meeting necessary?
- Who really needs to be there?
- What will be on the agenda?
- Who will be facilitating?
- What outcome are we seeking?
- Are there Minutes, and whose responsibility is it to take them?

Even if no Minutes are needed, action items should always be recorded and a follow-up email sent at the end of the meeting, listing who is responsible for each action point and the date it's due.

If the meeting is necessary, make sure the meeting has a **clear objective** by asking what the meeting is for.
- Is the meeting needed to generate new ideas or problem solve?
- Is it about getting together and gathering information?
- Is it to make decisions?
- Or is it a combination of all the above?

If you don't have a clear objective, you can be sure you won't accomplish much. If you are arranging these meetings for your executive, ask them what the clear objectives are. Now that you've got those questions answered, the next decision is what type of meeting you will schedule. Instead of the traditional congregating in a meeting room, consider the alternatives.

Outside meetings: Having a meeting outside the office can be a great idea, especially if only a few people are attending. This isn't an excuse to socialize; you still need an agenda and to meet the objectives. This is especially good when people are tired, usually in the afternoon. You could gather at a nearby café or a park. A change of scenery might help energize staff and may generate some good ideas.

Walk-and-talk meetings: I once worked for a company where we would have a 'walk-and-talk' meeting. This worked best with two people when you didn't need a laptop for the meeting. It was also a great way to get some exercise.

Stand-up meetings: These meetings are another way to get people to focus. Employees become more engaged, more collaborative, and less territorial when they participate in a project that involves standing. Nothing conveys urgency like being on your feet during a meeting. Stand-up meetings aren't always practical, but they're worth considering.

Zoom/Teams meetings: These have become the norm the past few years. These meetings may take place at home where there may be a lot of distractions. The best way to minimize distractions is preparation prior to your Zoom/Teams call. Make sure you are in an area of the home where you can focus, and there are minimum distractions.

Less is more: To get the best outcomes, invite only the key people. If you have too many people, especially people who don't need to be there, it is probable the meeting will not have the desired outcome. It is easier to focus on a decision with fewer people.

Late to a meeting: Do you know what is an acceptable time to be late to a meeting? If you said zero time, you are right. If a meeting is supposed to start at a certain time, start it. Starting right on time will send a clear message to those who are habitually late. Waiting for people can delay the time you finish or eat into someone's time to present. If you send the message that meetings will be starting on time, those latecomers will learn they need to be there on time and if not, they will stand out as always being the latecomers. Have a discussion with your executive about this... make sure you are both on board.

Don't lose focus: In meetings, sometimes there is that one person who tends to go off telling stories not connected to the discussed topic. And while storytelling is not generally bad, an off-topic discussion at a meeting can really drag the session and can steer it in the wrong direction.

The hardest task to accomplish leading a group of people is to get them to focus. Whether it's the organizer or any of the participants, someone should always take the responsibility of guiding the meeting back to the assigned topics and bringing back the focus.

Scope creep: This refers to constant uncontrollable changes in a meeting's scope. This can occur when the outcome of a project is not properly defined, documented, or controlled, and it is considered harmful for the success of a project. When a meeting has a clear focus, it's much easier to set concrete action steps and follow up. If you got to the end of the meeting without having actionable next steps, time has been wasted.

Multitasking: Don't multitask while you are in a meeting; actually, you should never multitask, because only 2% of the world's population is able to multitask. If you don't need to use your laptop or phone for the meeting, close your laptop and put your phone on silent until the meeting is complete. If you are distracted by reading emails or text messages in the meeting, you could miss important information.

Length: Unless there is a reason to have long meetings such as board meetings, then keep them short. Keep them around thirty to forty-five minutes and definitely don't go over an hour. The longer the meeting, the harder it is to keep your focus and keep your energy up. In all meetings, it is important to stick to the timing of the agenda and ask people to be prepared before they come into the meeting to present.

There are many ways companies like to hold their meetings, so if you are new, observe and take notes.

The Reason Why Meeting-Free Days Don't Work

When conducting a Google search there was a plethora of information about the benefits of implementing meeting free days and how productive they make you – but I disagree and I will explain why.

Sure, designating a day as meeting-free might indeed grant you a sense of productivity on that particular day. However, the real issue at hand, which can't be resolved by simply having one or two meeting-free days a week, revolves around the excessive scheduling of non-essential meetings. The problem we're facing is clear: we're dealing with an overwhelming influx of meetings, leading to a state of fatigue.

While the concept of reserving an entire day without meetings might seem like a solid idea on the surface, the execution doesn't always align seamlessly with the plan. In practice, this approach often ushers in unforeseen complications, particularly for assistants tasked with managing the schedules of busy executives. The crux of the matter remains that even without meetings on a specific day, the underlying issue of an excessive meeting load remains unresolved.

So, the solution isn't as straightforward as dedicating single days to be meeting-free. Instead, a more holistic approach is needed to tackle the root causes of meeting overload and the resulting burnout. The idea behind this concept is to create a day with no meetings, but what frequently happens is that all those meetings that were supposed to take place on that day simply get pushed to the other days. This ends up packing the calendar with a relentless stream of meetings, one after the other.

Instead of achieving a more organized and spacious schedule, what you often end up with is a jam-packed calendar that leaves little room for focused work or essential tasks. It's a classic case of good intentions leading to unintended consequences.

Rita Gunning

Working in a big multinational company means dealing with a bunch of crucial meetings spread across different time zones. Coordinating a meeting time with someone on the other side of the world while considering both their time and yours can be a juggling act. Now, imagine if you were limited to just four days to slot in these meetings. It's like an even bigger headache.

Some countries are way ahead or behind by hours, so what's Friday for one place could be Saturday for another. This twist can eat up another day when you're trying to plan things out. Handling all this in a huge company setup can be quite overwhelming.

It's also not a client friendly route to take; you are not being accommodating to the client by putting their meeting request off to another day because the day they are available is your meeting free day. That's not good for business. What if they too have implemented a meeting-free day that isn't the same day as the company you are working for? That now leaves three days to schedule a meeting.

I guess if you owned a very small company and everyone was in the same office, then meeting-free days might work.

Some meetings could be completely eliminated and replaced by emails, especially if it's regarding feedback about an issue or reporting where you are with a project. Sending emails instead of having meetings is a good option, but there has to be some structure around those emails; otherwise, you are spamming people's inbox by going back and forth about something that could be resolved with a quick phone call.

In my years of experience, what I found works best and is beneficial to do for yourself and your executive is block out times on the calendar as a no-meeting time; that way you can work on tasks without interruption, which makes you more productive.

These blocked times can be interchanged with rescheduled meetings. What I mean by that is... if a meeting needs to be rescheduled, there are times in the day that are blocked out as meeting-free times that can be swapped over based on the urgency of the meeting

Of course, there isn't a one-size-fits-all, and I don't believe there is a perfect method for anything in life, but we can work on making things simpler.

We have to stop jumping on the bandwagon of new trends such as meeting-free days. And while I'm on the topic of jumping on bandwagons - this is a side note; another one of the worst trends I have experienced in my working career is the open office.

There is absolutely no privacy in an open office, so to have a one-to-one with your executive or a private impromptu conversation about an issue with anyone, you have to book a meeting room, and these are usually limited. If those rooms are booked, you might have to go to a café with Wi-Fi in case you need to access your laptop - or you will need to wait until a meeting room becomes available.

In an open office situation, people tend to talk across the room; no one has their own partitioned desk area anymore - when you are working on a project or trying to concentrate, and people are talking across the room, it's distracting, and you may have to put off what you are doing until the office is quiet again. Before open offices, if you needed to speak to someone, you literally had to get up out of your seat and go to their cubicle.

Things Not to Do in a Meeting

Whether you like or dislike meetings, they are an essential part of the work environment; sometimes it's the best way to get things done. The best decisions come when the essential people congregate in a room to make those decisions or to brainstorm. However, there are things you shouldn't do in meetings, so I want to talk about the don'ts of the meeting etiquette world.

If you are scheduling a meeting, make sure it isn't a meeting that could be dealt with in an email. And the way to determine that is, if what you need is collaboration or you're waiting for feedback on an ongoing project, or you need to review deliverables from other team members, you don't need a meeting. These items can be addressed in an email.

Time is money, so be mindful of wasting yours and other people's time by scheduling meetings you don't need.

Here is a list of more things you shouldn't do in a meeting setting:

Turning up late: We can all agree that turning up late is a big no-no!!! It's annoying when you have to wait on someone, especially if that person is consistently late, try not to be judgemental in regard to those people; they might have a genuine issue with determining time. However, if I am facilitating a meeting, I wait three minutes after the start time and then I begin, whatever they miss is their loss.

Unprepared: It's so frustrating when there is a meeting scheduled to bring on a decision, but people come into the meeting unprepared, and they want to circle around the decision and waste time instead of putting something on the table for everyone to talk about. They end up derailing the meeting, which may result in another meeting needing to be scheduled. If a meeting was scheduled for a decision, then a resolution should be sought. So don't be that person who goes to a meeting unprepared.

Jargons & clichés: Using jargon and clichés to make yourself look more knowledgeable, when in fact you are really saying nothing at all, is annoying and frustrating. People can see straight through that. There is a saying that goes: "Better to remain silent and be thought a fool than to speak and to remove all doubt." - Abraham Lincoln

Noisy or smelly food: Sometimes meetings are scheduled during lunch (although they really shouldn't be), so people bring in their food to eat, and that's okay...but noisy foods such as apples or crisps (chips) should be avoided; people like me can find noise very distracting when trying to concentrate. Also avoid bringing in smelly foods, such as a tuna sandwich, because some people are sensitive to smells and are easily put off. If they are stuck inside a meeting room and can't escape, they will be more fixated on the smell than what is being said in the meeting.

Playing with devices: Playing with your phone, checking emails, or doing other work in meetings is disrespectful to the person talking. Give your full attention to that person, have your phone on silent, and unless you are taking notes, close your laptop.

Shutdown others: When someone suggests a solution to the topic being discussed, the worst thing you can do is just say it won't work and shut that thought down. You can state why you think it may not work and offer other suggestions or solutions, but just because you don't think something will work doesn't mean it won't! It's best you don't say anything at all.

Private conversations: If you are sitting in a meeting and someone else is talking, don't have a private conversation with the person sitting beside you or anyone else for that matter. One person should be talking at a time in a meeting; the others should be listening.

No agenda: There should always be an agenda; it should also have times corresponding to each item of the agenda. This will help the meeting keep on track. It's hard enough to keep on track with an agenda, can you imagine the chaos without one?

Keeping quiet: Don't be afraid to ask questions (unless it's a question that requires a lot of explanation, then take it offline because it might delay the meeting) and don't be afraid to give your input at a meeting, even if you are there to take Minutes. You never know, what you may say may help be the missing piece of a solution, or it might even be the whole solution, and if not, that's okay.

Icebreakers: For normal work meetings you don't need to add icebreakers; it makes the meeting go on too long, and some people, like me, hate icebreakers. It's more appropriate to have an icebreaker in a team-building situation rather than a meeting.

PART FOUR

Emails, Invites and Inbox, Oh My!

The Etiquette of Checking Meeting Availability

Throughout my years as an executive assistant, I've encountered instances where other executive assistants reach out via email to coordinate meetings for their respective executives. What frequently occurs is the lack of available dates and times provided in these communications. This can be frustrating, however, it's worth mentioning that some executive assistants might simply be unaware of the need to provide this information.

This situation can be attributed to a combination of reasons, ranging from oversight to a potential lack of understanding about the critical role that sharing available dates and times plays in the efficient scheduling of meetings. This difference in approaches highlights the diversity in practices among executive assistants across various situations.

Dealing with executive assistants who fail to provide available times for their executives' meetings can be frustrating. This lack of information necessitates extra effort on your part, essentially placing the onus on you to determine suitable meeting times and communicate them back via email. This often leads to unnecessary email exchanges that consume valuable time.

To streamline this process, when I initiate an email to another executive assistant inquiring about arranging a meeting between our respective executives, I always present my executive's available dates and times. These options are deliberately spread out across different days of the week or month, contingent on the urgency of the meeting. I lay out these dates and times in a clear bullet-point format.

Additionally, if there's no standard meeting location, I take the initiative to ask their preference in terms of meeting place. This query is presented with multiple options to choose from, including:

- Their office or
- Our office

- Zoom / Teams Meeting
- A nearby café that's convenient for them, as my executive is initiating the meeting and aims to accommodate the invitee's convenience.

These options are also structured in bullet-point format, facilitating easy selection. This approach not only expedites the process but also underscores the desire to collaborate and facilitate smooth decision-making.

Providing options within the same email as the available dates is an efficient approach that minimizes unnecessary email exchanges. By including the above location choices alongside the proposed meeting times, you empower the other executive assistant to review and assess whether any of the suggested dates align with their executive's schedule. This process enables them to quickly determine viable options and revert with their preferences, streamlining communication.

Once they've confirmed the dates that work and the preferred location, the responsibility then shifts to you to send out the official meeting invite. This approach not only reduces back-and-forth emails but also highlights a collaborative and effective manner of coordinating meetings. The expectation is for the inviting party to take charge of sending out the meeting invitation.

Questions and Update Email

The question and update email serves as an incredibly valuable tool in various scenarios and for different roles within the business landscape. It offers an efficient means of communication that can be used by:

Remote Workers Supporting an Executive: For remote employees tasked with assisting an executive, this email template becomes an indispensable tool to maintain effective communication and keep tasks on track.

Virtual Assistants: Virtual assistants, often working from different geographical locations, can leverage this email format to ensure they remain aligned with their clients and deliver efficient support despite the physical distance.

Time-Strapped Executives: Executives with packed schedules can still engage in meaningful communication with their executive assistants through this email approach. It provides a convenient means to address queries and provide updates amid a busy day.

Traveling Executives: For executives who are frequently on the move, this email template offers an excellent way to stay connected with their executive assistants, ensuring essential tasks and information are conveyed seamlessly, even when they're on the road.

The question and update email proves versatile in bridging communication gaps and facilitating effective collaboration among various professionals and scenarios within the business landscape.

The development of the question and update email technique stemmed from a practical necessity in my role as an executive assistant. At that time, I was supporting a managing director who frequently travelled to different states each week. While face-to-face catch-ups were feasible when he was in the same location, it became challenging to maintain effective communication when he was on the road, especially since video conferencing tools like Zoom were not yet widely available.

Complicating matters, he relied on a paper diary rather than digital tools, making it difficult for me to access his schedule. This limitation led me to create the questions and update email. In this email, I would inquire about his diary for the next day or two to gain insights into his schedule and meetings. When I did obtain this information, whether through viewing his diary or receiving updates via email, I would diligently update his Outlook calendar to reflect the upcoming meetings.

Another driving force behind this email method was the desire to streamline communication. Sending individual emails for various questions or updates ran the risk of getting lost in his inbox, which was a common issue. By consolidating all questions and updates into one email, I could ensure that he could address everything in a comprehensive manner.

Now, after a decade of using this approach, the process remains consistent. When my executive is traveling, I prepare a draft of the questions and update email for the day. This email serves as a repository for all questions and updates received in his inbox, including queries from others that require his attention. I typically send this email in the mid-morning, ensuring that it accounts for any correspondence received after my departure the previous day.

For executives with substantial time zone differences due to international travel, timing may vary. In such cases, sending the email just before leaving the office can align with their waking hours, potentially yielding quicker responses.

In situations where a matter is exceptionally urgent and requires immediate attention, I may resort to texting my executive and requesting a call when he is available. This method affords flexibility while ensuring critical issues are promptly addressed. Ultimately, the question and update email technique has proven its value in maintaining effective communication and collaboration in the ever-evolving landscape of executive support.

Below is an example of the questions and update email:

Hello Tom,

Please see the questions below that need your attention when you are free, and a few updates you should know before your return.

1. **Maryanne from Shelton House** *has finally got back to me regarding the catch up with both you and Tony and is* **asking about the scope of the meeting.**
2. *Nadia Harris has asked if we could* **move lunch with Michael Taylor from 13th July to 20th July** *because he won't be in the office that week,* **however on the 20th July you have;**
   a. *a* **Pipeline meeting** *with Jim that* **ends at 12noon,**
   b. *then* **lunch with Michelle at 12:30pm**
   c. **another pipeline meeting** *with Rachelle* **at 2pm**

   Did you want me to move all the meetings from a. to c. or *did you want me to* **see if Michael can do another day***. In saying that, your calendar is really busy for the month of July and you are also on leave.* **Waiting for instructions***.
2. *Just confirming you are* **still happy to fly back home the original time I booked***.
3. **ETL Agreement has been signed** *by their CEO,* **David Little,** *did you want me to* **add your signature?** *Who should I send it to besides Lauren?*

Updates
- *I have* **RSVP'd YES to** *the* **Tennis** *and invite has been received in your outlook calendar.* **Dinner first at Bartholomew Restaurant, King Street from 5:30pm** *and then Rugby at the SCC*
- *I am* **on leave today from 12noon** *and will be leaving my* **computer at work***, I will be in the office again tomorrow.*

You will notice in the email, the subject matter is questions and updates, and I include the date I'm sending the email. Within the email's body, two distinct headings outline the content. The first heading, "**Questions**," serves as a dedicated section for queries.

An interesting and practical aspect of this method is the use of numbered questions, rather than traditional bullet points. This numbering system simplifies your executive's responses. When your executive replies, they can simply reference the corresponding question number and provide their response. This approach streamlines communication, ensuring clarity and precision.

In cases where not all questions receive immediate answers, perhaps due to their complexity or the need for further investigation, your executive may indicate their intention to address these questions via a subsequent call. To ensure that these pending questions are not forgotten, a friendly reminder is included in the following questions and updates email.

The second heading, "**Update**," presents information that doesn't require a response. This content is structured using bullet points, conveying essential updates that require your executive's attention.

Another effective strategy incorporated into this email is the use of bolded words to draw attention to specific information. This approach facilitates quick scanning, ensuring that the highlighted words effectively convey key messages and action items. In essence, the bolded words create a concise narrative that guides your executive's focus and response, even when reading selectively.

Here are a few examples:

If you only read the words in bold, you will see it tells a story similar to reading the whole sentence.

4. **Maryanne from Shelton House** has finally got back to me regarding the catchup with both you and Tony and is **asking about the scope of the meeting.**

Bold words only: **Maryanne from Shelton House is asking about the scope of the meeting.**

As mentioned before, there are no numbers beside the updates only bullet points, if you want to go with numbers, then I suggest not to start from number one but start with the number after the last number you used in the 'Questions' section. This technique has been a valuable asset in my professional toolkit.

Helping Your Executive Manage Their Inbox

As executive assistants, we manage certain emails that arrive in our executive's inbox, while others are handled directly by the executive themselves. Occasionally, it can be challenging to encourage executives to promptly address their emails, resulting in an accumulation of messages within their inbox.

While some executives effectively stay on top of their email correspondence with minimal assistance, others may require more proactive support. Despite our efforts to remind them to respond to emails, it appears that certain executives continue to neglect this aspect, causing their inbox to become inundated.

The following techniques I am going to share are not a one-size-fits-all, so what works for one executive may not work for another. You may have to try a few of these techniques before you find the one that works for you and your executive.

Technique One:
- Prior to the catch-up meeting, take a moment to delete any irrelevant or spam emails in the inbox. This initial step helps declutter the inbox and focuses your attention on essential emails.
- Sit down with your executive and navigate through their inbox together. Respond to each email that requires immediate attention during this session.

- After responding to an email, promptly file it away into the appropriate folders or categories based on its nature or the action required. This ensures that actionable emails are organized and no longer occupy the inbox.
- For emails that do not necessitate immediate action but should be retained for reference, file them into a designated "Read Only" folder. This folder serves as an archive for emails that do not require an immediate response but may be relevant in the future.
- In cases where your executive is unable to read certain emails promptly, allocate time in one of your weekly catch-up meetings to review these emails together. This ensures that important messages are not overlooked and allows you to address them collectively.

Technique Two:
To effectively manage your executive's emails and ensure prompt responses, employ the following process:

- Prior to leaving work for the day, check your executive's email inbox for any new messages that have arrived since your morning catch-up. Make a list or note the details of emails that require your executive's attention.
- Upon arriving at work in the morning, perform a second check of your executive's inbox to identify any additional emails that may have come in overnight or early in the day. Note down the details of these emails.
- In your morning catch-up session with your executive, present the details of the new emails that have arrived since your last check. Read out the contents and any key information and note your executive's responses to each email.
- After concluding the catch-up meeting, immediately execute your executive's responses to each email.
- As you respond to each email, either delete it if it's no longer needed or file it into the appropriate folders for organized storage.

By following this technique, you maintain a proactive approach to managing your executive's emails.

Technique Three:
To enhance email organization and prioritize your executive's inbox, utilize a colour-coding system. Here's how to implement this technique effectively:

- Establish specific categories or colour codes for emails based on their urgency and purpose. For instance:
    - Red: Emails requiring immediate action.
    - Purple: Emails containing reading material or references.
    - Green: Emails that need your executive's attention but do not necessitate immediate action.

- Ensure your executive is aware of the color-coding system and understands its purpose. Discuss how it will help streamline email management and prioritize tasks.
- As emails arrive in your executive's inbox, assign the appropriate colour code to each one based on its content and urgency.
- The colour-coded system allows both you and your executive to quickly identify and prioritize emails. Red-coded emails, for example, signal urgent matters that need immediate attention, while purple-coded emails can be saved for later reading or reference.
- For red-coded emails requiring immediate action, prompt responses should be initiated. Once addressed, consider whether the email can be filed, deleted, or retained for reference.
- Purple-coded emails can be designated as reading material. You can allocate time for your executive to read and address these emails.
- Green-coded emails signal items that need your executive's attention but are not necessarily time-sensitive. These can be reviewed during designated periods for non-urgent tasks.

By implementing this colour-coding system, you create a visual aid for both you and your executive to efficiently manage email priorities and tasks.

Technique Four:
To improve your executive's email management and save them time, use this technique of scheduling:
- Work with your executive to determine the most suitable time slots for email review and management. This could be daily or several times a week.
- Schedule dedicated time slots in your executive's outlook calendar for email review. Depending on your executive's schedule, these appointments could be set up as recurring events to establish a consistent routine.
- In each outlook appointment, attach the emails that need your executive's attention during that specific time slot. These attachments serve as quick reference, allowing your executive to see the relevant emails directly within the calendar event.
- When attaching emails, provide brief contextual information or instructions related to each email. This helps your executive understand the purpose of reviewing these emails during the scheduled time.
- Configure reminder notifications for these email review appointments to ensure your executive is alerted when it's time to focus on their inbox.
- During the scheduled email review time, your executive can efficiently address, respond to, and organize their emails. Encourage them to utilize this time for productive email management.

By incorporating this technique, you enable your executive to proactively allocate time for email management and streamline their workflow.

Technique Five:
To efficiently manage and prioritize emails in your executive's inbox, implement a structured folder and reminder system:

- Set up dedicated folders within your executive's outlook inbox to categorize emails based on their status and action needed. Common folders include "To Be Read" and "To Be Actioned."
- Move incoming emails into the appropriate folders based on their content and urgency. For example:
  - Emails requiring reading or review go into the "To Be Read" folder.
  - Emails that need specific actions or responses are placed in the "To Be Actioned" folder.
- Utilize outlook email features to automate the sorting process. Configure rules to automatically direct certain types of emails to their respective folders, reducing manual sorting efforts.
- Create a recurring daily reminder in your executive's Outlook calendar to review the contents of these folders. Set the reminder for a convenient time when your executive can dedicate focused attention to email management.
- During the scheduled review time, your executive can address, respond to, or delegate emails as needed. Once an email has been read and actioned, it should be promptly removed from the "To Be Actioned" folder, either by filing it or deleting it.
- During your morning catch-up meetings, you can go over any remaining emails in the "To Be Read" and "To Be Actioned" folders, ensuring that nothing important is overlooked.

This structured folder and reminder system streamlines email management by providing a clear framework for categorizing and addressing emails.

Write Better Emails

I've encountered numerous poorly composed emails directed to either myself or my executive. These emails often feature lengthy and longwinded wording, leading to various interpretations depending on how they are read. I'd like to share some insights I've gathered over the years that have proven valuable in crafting effective emails.

Subject line: Don't add a subject line that is confusing. If there is a call to action, then add that in the subject line. For example: Subject: *Tom Brady's signature required on Broker Agreement Renewal*. The recipient of this email now knows what is required.

Add a greeting: Sometimes we get so preoccupied with the content of the email that we forget to add a greeting.

Prioritize clarity: Start by clearly stating the email's purpose. Use bullet points to highlight the key information or actions required in a concise manner.

Dear Sally,

I hope you are well.

Would you mind organizing the following please:

- *Tom signature on the attached broker agreement and returned to me by COB today.*

Then add the rest of the content.

I need this document signed by close of business today, please. A meeting has been scheduled with the broker tomorrow. The difference between this year's agreement and last year's agreement is that we've added a 2% increase in price.

Receiving a confusing wordy email: If you receive an email that's a little wordy and leaves you uncertain about the intended action; summarize your understanding of the sender's request and seek confirmation. Organize the summary in bullet points for clarity. This might require extra effort, it's better to get clarification than to proceed with the task, only to find what you did was incorrect. Sometimes when you take the time to summarize, you may work out the sender's intentions without the need for further confirmation.

Sending emails: When creating an email, don't make it too wordy. Break down each paragraph to two or three sentences. Make sure all the items needing attention are in bullet points.

Managing email threads with multiple 're' prefixes in the subject line: When dealing with an email thread that accumulates multiple "re" prefixes in the subject line due to ongoing communication, it's acceptable and advisable to streamline this by retaining just one "re." However, I recommend against altering the subject line to reflect the current content of the email thread. The original subject should be maintained for consistency. Avoid starting a new email for a topic that already has an existing email thread, as this can lead to confusion. Keep all relevant discussions within the same email thread to maintain clarity and context.

Adding or removing people from email threads: When you make changes to the recipients of an email thread, it's a good practice to include a note at the top of the email, enclosed in brackets, explaining who was added or removed and the reason for the change.

Treat your email as a draft: Prior to sending, it's essential to thoroughly review and revise your email. This process helps you identify grammatical and spelling errors, as well as fine-tune the tone and content.

Avoid criticising suggestions: Rather than simply rejecting ideas, especially in email communication, promote constructive feedback and suggestions. Maintain a positive and encouraging tone when addressing proposals or contributions.

PART FIVE

The Daily Grind

How to Deal with Conflicting Priorities

Dealing with conflicting priorities is a common challenge that many of us face in our personal and professional lives. It can be overwhelming and stressful to balance competing demands, but there are strategies that can help you manage conflicting priorities effectively.

Prioritize and organize: One of the first steps to addressing conflicting priorities is to identify which tasks are urgent and which can wait. Make a list of all the tasks you need to complete and the deadlines assigned to each one. Then categorize them based on their level of importance, urgency of the task, and the tasks that may cost the company money if they are not completed on time. This will help you focus on the tasks that are most critical and ensure you are not missing any crucial deadlines.

Communicate with others: If you are working with a team, it is important to communicate priorities and discuss any potential conflicts. This will help you identify any areas where you can delegate tasks or collaborate with others to achieve your goals. Communication is key to ensuring everyone is on the same page and your team is working together towards a common goal.

Learn to say no: This is hard to do because you may fear that your job may be at risk, or you have a hard time saying no because you don't want to let anyone down, but you are letting yourself down if you don't say no. Sometimes, conflicting priorities may arise because you have taken on too much work. It is important to know your limits and learn to say no when you are already overloaded. This will help you avoid taking on more tasks than you can handle and reduce the likelihood of conflicts arising in the future.

Be flexible: In some cases, conflicting priorities may require you to be flexible and adapt to changing circumstances. This may involve adjusting your schedule or re-prioritizing tasks based on new information. Being open to change and willing to adapt can help you navigate conflicting priorities more effectively.

Take breaks: When you are dealing with conflicting priorities, it can be overwhelming and stressful. It happens to the best of us. Taking regular breaks can help you recharge and stay focused. This could involve taking a short walk, doing a quick workout, or simply stepping away from your work for a few minutes. One thing I also recommend is to always take your lunch break. Don't sit at your desk and work while you eat, take the time to enjoy your lunch.

Use technology to your advantage: In this day and age there are so many tools and apps available to us that can help to manage priorities more effectively. For example, you could use a task management app to keep track of your to-do list and even enable notifications to receive reminders for certain tasks coming up. You can even use your calendar app to schedule your work and personal commitments. These tools can help you stay organized and ensure you are not missing any important deadlines or upcoming engagements.

Practice self-care: It is important to take care of yourself. This may involve getting enough sleep, eating a healthy diet, and engaging in activities you enjoy. When you are feeling your best, you are better equipped to handle the challenges that come with balancing competing demands.

Dealing with conflicting priorities can be a challenge, but with the right strategies, it is possible to manage them effectively. So, by prioritizing and organizing your tasks, communicating with others, learning to say no, being flexible, taking breaks, using technology to your advantage, and practicing self-care, you can minimize stress and achieve your goals.

Conquer Overwhelm and Boost Your Productivity

Feeling overwhelmed is part of what makes us human, and sometimes it can be paralysing. When you're overwhelmed, it can be difficult to know where to start or what to do next.

Being overwhelmed is a feeling, and it's brought on by thoughts. You think you don't have control of the way you feel due to your circumstances, but this is not true, even though your circumstance has triggered these feelings, you do have control.

When you feel overwhelmed, you are telling yourself a story: It's all too much. You don't have time to do this. You can't handle it. You don't know where to start. You don't know what to do. When you are in this mindset, it's hard to take action, so you continue to replay this story in your mind, which keeps you in that emotion of being overwhelmed. This, my friend, becomes a vicious cycle.

Being overwhelmed can make you become withdrawn, fatigued, irrational, confused, and sick. However, there are several strategies you can use to change the way you think.

Acceptance: Accept you are feeling overwhelmed because of your thoughts. Do all you can to get some perspective on the situation. Talk it out, write it down, go for a walk, meditate, or do anything beneficial that comforts you. It will help to gather your thoughts.

Don't make assumptions: Don't jump too far ahead of yourself in regard to what you think is going to happen because of your circumstance. Most of the time, your assumptions are false. Your worst fears are never realized, and the situation turns out much better than you thought.

Stop looking at the big picture, such as all the deadlines you need to meet or your list of things to do, and start thinking of the steps you need to take to get things done.

Prioritize your tasks: One of the most effective ways to overcome overwhelm is to prioritize your tasks. This means taking a step back and assessing what needs to be done and then deciding which tasks are most important. You can use a to-do list or a task management software to help you prioritize. Once you have a clear idea of what needs to be done, you can start tackling the most important tasks first.

Break tasks into smaller steps: Sometimes tasks can feel overwhelming because they are too big or complex. If this is the case, try breaking the task down into smaller steps. This can make the task feel more manageable and help you make progress. For example, if you need to write a report, break it down into research, outlining, drafting, and editing. Focus on one step at a time. You'd be surprised how quickly you make progress.

Eliminate distractions: Distractions can be a major source of overwhelm. If you find yourself constantly checking your phone, email, or social media, try eliminating these distractions. Turn off notifications, put your phone on silent and put it in a drawer. You'll be amazed how much more focused you can be without these distractions.

Ask for help: If you're feeling overwhelmed, it's okay to ask for help. Whether it's delegating tasks to a colleague or hiring a professional to assist with a project, getting help can make a big difference. Don't be afraid to reach out to others and ask for support.

Learn to say NO: If you don't have the luxury of getting help, learn to say NO or push back on tasks or deadlines. Those who do more get rewarded less by being given more. That has been my personal experience. Saying NO gets easier the more you say it.

Practice self-care: When you're overwhelmed, it can be easy to neglect self-care. However, taking care of yourself is essential for managing overwhelm. Make sure you're getting enough sleep, eating well, and getting regular exercise. Take breaks throughout the day to recharge and prioritize activities that bring you joy. By not practicing self-care the likelihood of you becoming overwhelmed increases.

I'm not saying these things I have suggested are easy, to be perfectly honest they are not, but when you feel overwhelmed, recognize and accept the feeling and the situation you are in and then follow what I have suggested.

Working a Room, a.k.a. Small Talk

I've been involved in coordinating and participating in numerous charitable, social, staff, and client events across various countries. These occasions often require me to engage with attendees, initiate conversations, and engage in small talk. However, it's common for many individuals to feel apprehensive about these tasks, even if they're integral to the role of an executive assistant.

Despite it being a part of our job, many of us may lack confidence when it comes to working the room. This self-doubt often stems from what's known as 'impostor syndrome,' where we feel like we're not genuine and worry that others won't find our contributions interesting. I'll delve deeper into addressing this syndrome shortly.

Before any event, I consciously prepare my mindset for the meet-and-greet. I choose an outfit that I genuinely like and feel comfortable in because, as the saying goes, "when you look good, you feel good," and this boost in confidence empowers me. It's like feeling ready to take on the world.

I've always preferred taking the initiative. I approach people and introduce myself with a brief summary of who I am. Taking this proactive role significantly enhances my self-assurance.

Keep in mind that you should always feel comfortable with your approach while maintaining utmost respect.

Admittedly, when I initially started working a room, I wasn't particularly skilled at it. However, over the years, it has become second nature. My so-called success in working a room can be attributed to my strategy of having a broad knowledge base on various topics and a deep understanding of subjects that genuinely pique my interest.

Here are some things you can do to learn a little about a lot:
- If you can, go travelling; it opens your mind to new experiences.
- If you are not able to travel, then watch YouTube videos on countries you would like to visit and their culture. The person you may be talking to at an event may come from that country or just visited the country, so you have a topic to talk about.
- Watch documentaries or videos on topics you find interesting. There are a lot of documentaries on YouTube and streaming services.
- Read about interesting topics and stay away from discussing politics and religion.
- Show genuine interest in other people's conversations; there's a wealth of knowledge to gain from doing so. In many cases, people enjoy speaking more than listening, so actively listen and pose open-ended questions. When you're ready to conclude the conversation and transition, switch to closed-ended questions.
- Don't spend too long with one person if you need to work the room; politely excuse yourself and let them know you need to greet a few more people, and it was lovely to meet them. Don't make excuses like you need to get another drink or you need to use the bathroom. If the person is alone, introduce them to someone else before you leave.

Small talk can be arduous at times, but it could lead to great conversations, great friendships, and is definitely a great way to network.

Impostor Syndrome

Impostor syndrome meaning: a psychological pattern in which an individual doubts their skills, talents, or accomplishments and has a persistent internalized fear of being exposed as a fraud. (Wikipedia)

Two American psychologists, Pauline Clance and Suzanne Imes, came up with that name in 1978. They described it as a feeling of phoniness in people who believe they are unintelligent, incapable, or uncreative despite evidence of high achievement. While these people are highly motivated to achieve, they also live in fear of being 'found out' or exposed as frauds.

No one is immune from imposter syndrome, and people experience it across all levels and industries. There are very successful people who head big companies who have felt it at one time or another.

There is a quote by Richard Branson that goes like this:

> *"If someone offers you an amazing opportunity, but you are not sure you can do it, say yes – then learn how to do it later!"*

This quote, in my interpretation, highlights that despite Richard's lack of initial knowledge when faced with opportunities, he embraced the challenges and acquired expertise through experience. It's a valuable lesson for all of us.

For a significant duration of my career as an executive assistant, I grappled with feelings of being an impostor, particularly when I embarked on a new position within a different company. During meetings, I'd have feelings of inadequacy as I struggled to comprehend the discussions around me. I feared that maybe I was not cut out for the role, and that sooner or later, my inadequacy would be exposed.

However, over the years and after numerous conversations with colleagues and friends from all walks of life and positions, I came to realize that these feelings are more common than I initially believed. It's not limited to executive assistants but extends across various roles, especially when one joins a new organization.

The truth is every company operates differently and employs unique terminologies. They often undertake projects with names that might seem cryptic to newcomers. Therefore, during the initial stages of your employment, while you're still getting familiarized and learning about the company, its people and their ongoing projects, it's crucial to be compassionate toward yourself.

In our minds, we think we only know a little bit, and everyone else knows so much more, but the reality is, we all know the same but about different things.

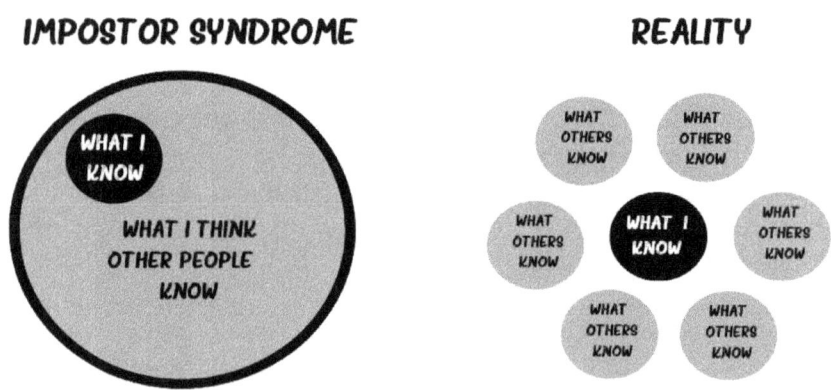

Imposter syndrome can manifest in different ways, and here are some examples:
- difficulty accepting praise and recognition for personal accomplishments.
- reluctance to seize opportunities and take initiative.

- reluctance to accept promotions or new assignments because of not feeling 'ready'.
- reluctance to highlight personal contributions to projects.
- trouble delegating, due to a need to ensure everything is done to impossibly high standards.
- individualism and a difficulty accepting help.
- procrastination caused by an immobilizing fear of failure.
- workaholism stemming from a feeling of incompetence and a perceived need to work harder.

If you find yourself relating to any or most of these feelings, don't worry; you're not alone. You might wonder what to do about it. As executive assistants, we're constantly learning and thinking on our feet. To combat imposter syndrome during meetings, consider taking thorough notes. After meetings, don't hesitate to ask your colleagues for clarification on topics you found challenging, and for other issues, conduct some research.

Remember that no one starts out knowing everything; ongoing learning is key. There will be times when you stumble, but the goal is to persist and embrace failures as opportunities for growth. Reflect on your achievements in your role and maintain a success log, not only for self-encouragement but also for discussing your accomplishments during your year-end performance review.

When someone praises you, graciously accept their compliments without downplaying your achievements. Getting out of your comfort zone is essential for personal growth; staying stagnant won't help you progress.

If you're offered a project or promotion that pushes you beyond your comfort zone, trust the judgment of those who recommended you. They saw potential in you that you might not have recognized in yourself. Opportunities like these don't come around every day, so seize them. Invest in research and skill development to excel in your new role. Pursue your aspirations; your chances of success are just as good as anyone else's, even if it means putting in some extra effort in research or skill-building.

When you are feeling like a fraud or feeling overwhelmed about doing something, acknowledge what you are feeling is impostor syndrome and it's a real feeling, but remind yourself you got this, and you are not alone. By the way, having a little bit of impostor syndrome isn't a bad thing; it keeps you grounded.

The Myth of Multitasking

In the role of an assistant, there is a myth that you should be able to multitask. When you look at an executive assistant or an admin assistant's position description, one of the skills employers ask for is 'someone who can multitask.'

As Wikipedia puts it: "multitasking is the concept that one can split their attention on more than one task or activity at the same time, such as singing with the song on the radio while driving a car."

A study from the University of Bergen in Norway, shows that multitasking takes a serious toll on productivity. Your brain lacks the ability to perform multiple tasks at the same time. The study found that about 2.5% of people are what are called "supertaskers" and are able to efficiently work through multiple problems at once. The other 97.5% don't have this ability. In moments where you think you are multitasking; you are really only switching from task to task.

While most of us can do two simple tasks at the same time, such as walking and chewing gum, the same can't be said for more complex tasks. The modern workplace is designed to promote multitasking. You've been sold a lie that you're more efficient when you try to do multiple things at once. But this isn't the case; your efficiency can drop by as much as 40%.

Each time you switch activities, your brain is being forced to go through two energy-intensive stages:
- First stage is goal shifting. This is where you decide to do one thing instead of another.
- Second stage is role activation. This is where you change from the rules or context of the previous task to the new one.

The absolute power and efficiency come from single-tasking; but what is single-tasking?

Wikipedia states: "Single tasking is the practice of dedicating oneself to a given task and minimizing potential interruptions until the task is completed or a significant period of time has elapsed."

If you want to get tasks done at a higher quality and in less time, then it pays to focus on one thing at a time, and here's why.
- Single tasking makes the task less stressful because you are more likely to get into a state of flow and finish what you set out to do.
- Single tasking makes you focus on what you "should" do rather than what you "could" do.

Here are some steps that lead to better efficiency:

Each day:
- Create a daily schedule with dedicated time for focused work. If you can prepare for your tomorrow the day before, it will make this process even more efficient.
- Block out between thirty to forty-five minutes in the calendar for each task and concentrate on that one task.
- Even the task of checking your emails should have time allocated, or you might find yourself checking when you are completing another task, therefore multitasking and decreasing productivity.
- Did you know it takes an average of fifteen minutes to reorientate to a primary task after a distraction such as an email?

- Put your phone on silent and log yourself out of the tools and websites you don't need at the time of performing a certain task.
- Find a quiet place, a place with limited distractions so the task at hand can be completed.

By the way, both men and women are equally bad at multitasking. As researchers from the University of Bergen in Norway write:
"We cannot exclude the possibility that there are no sex differences in serial multitasking abilities, but if they do exist, such differences are likely to be very small."

Stay on Top of Your tasks with a Notebook:

If you're similar to me, once you finish a task, you tend to move forward without dwelling on it because there's always so much to tackle. However, when my executive inquires about the results of something I was working on a month ago, I can easily reference my notebook to provide them with precise details.

The technique: During my catch-up sessions with my executive, I consistently bring along my notebook. For this technique, I come prepared with both a black and a blue pen, and I also find it beneficial to have a red pen and a yellow highlighter on hand. I've personally developed and refined this approach over my thirty years of experience, and it has proven highly effective for me.

Here is the breakdown of the purpose for each colour:
- The black pen is used to write down not only the requests from my executive but also used to write down any queries I have, emails that have come in for my executive I need to address, or staff members' questions I need my executive's input on.

- The blue pen is used to show I have started on the task but am waiting on something else to happen before I can move on.
- The red pen is used to detail the final step I took to close off the task.
- The yellow highlighter is used to show that this task is completed, and I can move on.

Okay, so let me give you some scenarios to help you visualize this concept:

I'm getting ready for a meeting with my executive. I grab my notebook and jot down today's date. Equipped with both my blue and black pens, I head into the meeting. During our discussion, my executive assigns me three tasks, and I've got a pressing question of my own to ask.

Here are the three tasks my executive entrusts to me:

1. Secure airport parking.
2. Send an email over to Tom Jones to schedule a quarterly meeting at their office next month.
3. Should a specific report from a client not arrive at the beginning of the month, I'm to remind my executive midway to follow up with that client via a phone call.

Now, for my question to my executive:

I inquire about which calendar invites, scheduled for the upcoming week, should be accepted or declined. In my notebook, I meticulously list the invite details, including:
- Dates
- Times
- Subject matter
- Sender

Next to each entry in red, I mark either a 'Y' for accept or an 'N' for decline. Later, I either update these requests on my laptop or, if I'm viewing the invites alongside my executive, I promptly accept or decline each one there and then.

Task one: Book parking at the airport. Prior to making the parking reservation, I carefully review the e-ticket to ascertain the departure and arrival dates and times. For domestic flights, I schedule the car park check-in a minimum of two hours before my executive's departure and the check-out two hours after their flight's arrival. This buffer time accommodates any potential flight delays. In the case of international flights, I book the check-in four hours before the departure and three hours after the scheduled arrival.

Once the reservations are secured, I record the booking times and associated confirmation number in my notebook using a red pen. These details are also promptly added to my executive's Outlook calendar, complete with the reservation confirmation attachment. Once this task is successfully accomplished, I highlight the task in my notebook in yellow which marks it as complete.

Task two: When my executive tasks me with setting up a quarterly meeting at Tom Jones' office for the upcoming month, the process unfolds like this:

If Tom has an executive assistant, my first step is to reach out to them. I inquire about Tom's availability for the quarterly meeting and provide them with a range of dates and times when my executive is available to meet. This will assist them in finding a suitable time and inform me in their response. I write down the times I provided to Tom's executive assistant in my notebook using a blue pen.

However, if Tom doesn't have an executive assistant, I directly contact him via email. I share my executive's available dates and times. I write down the times I provided Tom in my notebook using a blue pen.

I patiently await a response, whether from Tom himself or his executive assistant. Once I receive their reply, I use a red pen to document the outcome. For instance:

- Tom's EA responded with Tom's availability for February 20th at 10 a.m.
- I proceed to send the invitation, designating Tom's office as the meeting location.
- To ensure my executive is informed, I relay the details to them and mark this task as complete by highlighting it in yellow.

Task three: Reminding my executive to follow up with a client in the middle of the month if a report doesn't come in. I make sure to set a reminder for myself in my calendar for the middle of the following month to ensure I don't forget. Additionally, I also consider adding this reminder to my executive's calendar for their awareness.

In blue pen, I document that I've set a reminder in my calendar, including the specific date and time it's scheduled for. However, I don't take any further action until the expected report arrives. If the report does arrive on time, I make a note in red pen of the date it was received, then remove the follow-up reminder from both my calendar and my executive's. I highlight this task in yellow to signify its completion.

If, by the time my reminder is set, the report hasn't arrived, I bring this to my executive's attention during our next catchup. Once I've informed my executive, I document in red pen that I reminded them to call the client. I withhold highlighting this task in yellow until it's fully resolved.

It's a good practice to periodically flip back through my notebook's pages to ensure all tasks are highlighted. If there are tasks that remain unhighlighted, I review them to determine if they need follow-up or more time. In case further action is required, I document the details in red pen before eventually marking it as completed with a yellow highlighter.

Plan for Tomorrow, Today!

At the end of your workday before you go home, spend the last fifteen minutes planning for tomorrow. From your list of things to do, identify the three most important things you need to do the next day and schedule time on your calendar to do those things as soon as you start your workday. Make a list of the things you need to discuss with your executive at your catchup. If you are working on a big project, don't make the mistake of listing a big project as one item. Instead, break it down into smaller tasks and add three of those tasks to your list of things to do the next day. Allocate time in your calendar for each of those tasks.

When writing down your tasks, be specific; for example: Don't write '*call accounts*' because you may forget why; instead, write '*call accounts department to see if xyz have paid their invoice.*' This will make things clear, and you won't waste time trying to remember what you needed to do.

Productive people do the most important things first. The way to be sure they are completing the most important things is to plan for them and make a conscious decision to work on them. Plan for your tomorrow, today. Be intentional, not reactional.

PART SIX

Dirty Laundry

"I'm not interested in what you have to say!"
he yelled at me while pointing his index finger in my face.
"What you say doesn't interest me at all; your job is to do as I say!"

My new managing director said this to me three weeks into his role at the company where I was already employed. While it wasn't the first time he had been rude to me, it certainly was the last.

I had been working at the company for a year and an executive assistant for over twenty-five years by this stage, and no one had ever spoken to me that way. I was shocked! What had I done wrong? I had been more than helpful with his transition into the company. It came to my attention later that it wasn't anything I had done wrong. He simply wanted to make me so uncomfortable that I would leave – and he could employ his former executive assistant.

I refused to back down and firmly told him that I would not tolerate being spoken to that way again. In response, I arranged a meeting with my executive and the HR manager. During that meeting, I made it clear that if they wished to part ways with me, they would have to provide a substantial redundancy package. Otherwise, they would be facing a potential bullying case.

Ultimately, I did receive a good redundancy payout and left the company. However, it was a bittersweet victory because I had to leave a job I had once loved.

Being an executive assistant can be incredibly rewarding when you work with the right executive. However, there are times when the experience can be challenging and unpleasant. In this chapter of the book, I want to shed light on some of the less pleasant aspects of being an executive assistant. Just bear with me while I air out some dirty laundry and then continue with the good stuff.

Rita Gunning

Things I Dislike About Being an Executive Assistant

As executive assistants, we seem to be afraid of telling it like it is. We fear talking about the parts of our role we don't like, and we think that somehow by mentioning these things, we will be judged as being incompetent.

I've been an executive assistant for thirty years, which should suggest I still enjoy the role, but some days and some companies have really highlighted what I don't like about this position and here are some examples.

Maid service: This is often a component of our job to a certain degree. For external client meetings held in our office, we provide beverages and coordinate catering. Additionally, we are responsible for tidying up the meeting room after their departure. However, we shouldn't be required to provide this level of service to our colleagues. Yet, in certain companies, it appears to be an expectation.

Last-minute gift buying: We are tasked with buying last-minute gifts. Sometimes it's for individuals we don't really know, and we are not given any guidance as to what they like so it falls on us to figure it out.

Mind reading: We are expected to know about everything that's going on, even though we haven't been included in the meetings or the private conversations.

Scape goat: We are sometimes blamed for things that go wrong even if we had nothing to do with it.

Service for hire: Certain executives may extend our services to colleagues who are facing challenges, regardless of whether that colleague is inefficient or lacks motivation. I recall a situation where I was requested to provide Excel graph creation lessons to an accountant. Yes, you heard correctly, I had to teach an accountant how to create graphs.

IT technician: In the event of software or hardware issues, we are often the initial point of contact for our executive, even when a competent IT team is available. Some executives prefer us to attempt a quick resolution before involving IT. I've found YouTube to be a valuable resource for troubleshooting IT problems.

Genius: We are expected to have answers for everything – even if it's not within our expertise.

Above and beyond: We work beyond our job description, which keeps growing and growing.

Mistakes get highlighted: Given that we handle tasks for numerous individuals, any mistakes we make tend to stand out because our work is reviewed by a larger audience. In contrast, some other roles involve individual work, where errors may not be as readily noticed.

Human punching bag: Certain executives display inappropriate behaviour by directing their emotions, particularly when stressed or behaving rudely, towards us. They may raise their voices when things don't go their way, give us the cold shoulder, or, in extreme cases, even display physical outbursts. Some executive assistant blogs may suggest developing a thick skin to tolerate such behaviour, but I firmly disagree. This type of conduct is entirely unacceptable.

Tea lady: Getting your executive's coffee or lunch when they are genuinely busy is completely fine, and it's a thoughtful gesture. However, I strongly disagree with an executive requesting you to fetch their lunch when they are not occupied but simply can't be bothered to go out themselves.

Going solo: In some of my past workplaces, I've been the sole executive assistant, and it has posed challenges. It can be tough because while everyone belongs to a specific department, I didn't have one, so when departments went out for lunch, I often found myself excluded, and that was disheartening.

Fighting for your worth: During performance reviews, assessing our Key Performance Indicators (KPIs) can be challenging. Our work often involves quick reactions and a fast-paced environment, which can make it difficult to clearly quantify our achievements. Even when we efficiently support our executives and streamline their roles, it's often challenging to demonstrate the background efforts that contribute to their day-to-day success. This can make it tough to convey our true value.

Dealing with Difficult Executives

At times, executive assistants are faced with challenging executives. Many of you have likely encountered executives who make it difficult to work with. For instance:

- They consistently find fault in your work, regardless of your efforts.
- They struggle to articulate their needs clearly but hold you accountable for not anticipating their wishes.
- They exhibit uncertainty about their requirements, yet they expect you to discern them, and even when you create what you believe they need, they express dissatisfaction.
- They keep you in the dark about crucial matters you should be aware of. They exclude you from meetings where your presence is vital, or they neglect to share the meeting outcomes. And yet, they anticipate you to respond on their behalf regarding these matters.

In such situations, it can be challenging to showcase your capabilities. I'm certain many of you can contribute more examples based on your own encounters. If you haven't encountered such difficult executives, consider yourself fortunate.

Here are some recommendations for handling these challenging executives, based on my past experiences:

- Approach interactions with professionalism and politeness, even when faced with difficulty. It's crucial to remain composed, as escalation can be detrimental. Remember that, despite the circumstances, these executives may hold more power within the organization.
- Pay close attention to understand their needs and frustrations thoroughly. There might be aspects of your work that you're unaware of causing issues. Seek clarity by confirming your understanding of their needs through questions. Stay receptive to constructive feedback, as everyone has professional blind spots.
- Be flexible and willing to explore different approaches. If a particular method isn't effective, consider trying an alternative tactic. Propose solutions that benefit both parties.
- When asked, provide feedback in a constructive manner. Focus on solutions rather than criticism, as criticism can create division. Concentrate on addressing the current issue and avoid delving into past grievances. Maintain transparency and honesty in communication, being mindful of your body language and tone.
- Document conversations for future reference. Writing things down aids memory retention and serves as a reference point. In case of accusations of wrongdoing, having documentation can demonstrate what was discussed.
- Try not to take things personally and strive to maintain a positive outlook. While this can be challenging, particularly if you feel singled out, it's essential not to internalize negativity.

If you've exhausted these strategies and the situation continues to negatively impact your job satisfaction, leading to anxiety and stress, it may be time to consider seeking another job. No one should tolerate an environment that makes them feel this way. Every individual deserves to be treated with respect, regardless of their position in a company.

If you are experiencing workplace bullying and/or sexual harassment, it's essential to speak up and take action. Report any incidents of bullying or harassment to your human resources department. Such behaviour should never be tolerated in the workplace. Keep a record of each instance of harassment or bullying by making notes. Send these notes to your personal email; they can serve as documentation if the situation escalates. Bring this matter to the attention of your HR manager.

Regarding difficult executives who are not engaging in bullying or harassment, in most cases, there may be limited recourse. Often, HR tends to support executives because they can be challenging to replace. However, it's crucial to remember that no job should compromise your mental health and safety. Prioritize your well-being above all else.

Unusual Things I've Been Asked to do as an Executive Assistant

I've encountered some unusual requests from executives that went well beyond my job description. Interestingly, the first three peculiar requests all came from the same CEO during my time at a finance company.

Company mascot: My executive once requested that I put on our company's mascot costume and engage with passers-by on the street. It happened to be an exceptionally sweltering day, and I was fully enclosed in the costume, including a helmet that served as the mascot's head. The experience was incredibly uncomfortable, and I felt like I might suffocate in the heat. When asked to do it a second time on a different occasion, I firmly declined. I had no intention of repeating that unpleasant experience.

Side hustle: The individual who crafted our company's mascot outfit ran a tailoring business in Thailand. Consequently, my executive had the idea of starting a side hustle by offering to create men's suits and shirts for our staff members. He wanted me to learn how to take measurements so we could send the orders to Thailand. One of the measurements I was expected to take involved measuring the inner thigh of male staff members, which required measuring from the crotch area downward. I respectfully declined, citing the inappropriateness of the request, considering that we were both employed by a finance company, not a tailoring business.

Making bacon: One evening, as I was about to leave work, my executive called me into his office and requested that I prepare breakfast for all the staff members in the building the following day. That was a total of 75 people. It meant I had to stop by the supermarket on my way home to buy the necessary ingredients and then arrive at work early the next morning to prepare and cook. I ended up making scrambled eggs on toast with fried tomatoes and bacon. On another occasion, I was asked to prepare bruschetta. I must have missed the part about being the resident chef in my job description.

Plagiarizing: During my time at an international school in Asia, I encountered an unsettling situation involving my executive, who held the position of assistant headmaster. He would target single mothers among the teaching staff and request that they meticulously create a teaching program for the upcoming summer school. The premise was that they would be responsible for instructing the program and receive compensation for their work. Regrettably, the executive would proceed to plagiarize their program and bring his son, a teacher in the United States, to Asia to deliver the curriculum that someone else had authored. This was a deeply unethical practice that understandably caused distress among the affected teachers.

The teacher who had assembled the program was well aware of my executive's unethical actions but felt powerless to report them due to the fear of losing her job. Unfortunately, my executive was engaged in numerous activities that were either illegal or violated company policies. I remained at the school for slightly over a year, and in my final weeks there, I gathered documentation and reported my executive's misconduct to the board members. However, my efforts to shed light on these issues were met with resistance, and I was unfairly portrayed as the instigator. I quickly realized that the organization had a culture that protected certain individuals (mainly men – it was a boys club), and my concerns and the evidence I presented were ultimately disregarded.

The affair: I discovered that my executive was involved in an affair with someone from a different department on a separate floor within our workplace. I accidentally came across an email that he hastily deleted once he realized I had seen it, but by then, it was too late. I couldn't erase what I had seen, and he was aware of that fact. As a result, he requested that I keep this information to myself. I never disclosed it to anyone, not a soul. I had a friendly rapport with my executive's wife, as she would often drop by our workplace before going to lunch with her husband. Whenever she visited, we would engage in pleasant conversations.

Over time, his wife began to suspect that her husband might be having an affair. She would occasionally call me to seek confirmation of her suspicions. I had to dissemble and pretend that I had no knowledge of what she was talking about. I encouraged her to address her concerns directly with her husband, as I could not confirm or deny anything. A few weeks later, she called me and accused me of being the one involved in an affair with her husband. I repeatedly assured her that this was not the case, but the situation escalated, and office gossip began circulating rumours that I was the one having the affair with my executive. I reached a breaking point and informed my executive that he needed to come clean with his wife, or I would do so, as I had been unwillingly drawn into this mess. Eventually, he did confess to his wife. I believe the affair ended, and his wife chose to stay with him. I, on the other hand, decided to move on to another company.

Since that incident, I've become cautious about being overly friendly with my executives. I maintain a pleasant demeanour, engage in light banter, but I am careful to protect myself from being entangled in such situations again.

The chicken pesto salad debacle: I once had an executive who frequently asked me to fetch her lunch, even when she wasn't particularly busy. On one occasion, she requested a chicken pesto salad without specifying where to purchase it. However, I was aware that the place where I often bought my lunch offered chicken pesto salads. I returned to the office and handed her the salad, but to my surprise, she expressed dissatisfaction. As it turned out, the salad I had brought her wasn't the one she preferred. She actually wanted me to go to a cafe located a ten-minute walk away from the office, which would have consumed twenty minutes of my own lunch hour. It's worth noting that she didn't have any meetings scheduled around her lunchtime that day.

Reluctantly, I headed out again to acquire the salad she wanted from the cafe. Consequently, I found myself in possession of the initial chicken pesto salad I had purchased but couldn't consume, so I ended up giving it away.

These are just a few examples of the many unusual experiences I've had throughout my career, but I'm sure you probably have your own share of peculiar requests and stories to tell.

PART SEVEN

Checklists Are for Winners

The Importance of Having a Checklist

As an executive assistant, I've discovered the value of having a checklist for several reasons:

- Checklists help keep tasks organized and ensure nothing important is overlooked.
- They assist in prioritizing tasks, ensuring that the most critical ones are addressed first.
- By following a checklist, I can work more efficiently, reducing the chances of wasting time on less important tasks.
- Checklists provide a clear plan, reducing stress and anxiety associated with managing multiple tasks.
- They help track progress and hold me accountable for completing tasks.
- Checklists are also useful for communicating task progress with my executive or team.
- They promote consistency in handling recurring tasks or processes.
- I can adapt checklists to different projects or situations, making them versatile tools.
- They serve as a record of completed tasks, which can be useful for reference or reporting.
- Regularly using checklists allows for continuous improvement by refining processes and identifying areas for optimization.

In essence, checklists are indispensable tools for maintaining organization, efficiency, and effectiveness as an executive assistant. They can truly elevate your performance in this role, making you a Superstar executive assistant. Of course, the specific checklists you use can vary depending on your responsibilities. Let's delve deeper into this concept.

The primary checklist to start with is your daily schedule. It should encompass all your daily activities, including tasks like calendar management for both you and your executive.

Depending on your daily tasks, you might have different checklists for different days, tailored to specific responsibilities.

As you establish a routine with your daily checklist, these tasks will become second nature, and you'll find yourself relying on this checklist less frequently. It's crucial to distinguish your to-do list from your checklists; they serve distinct purposes.

Moving on to the second checklist, we have the 'Organizing Events' checklist. Since event planning isn't an everyday occurrence, having a dedicated checklist for this purpose is invaluable. I've included a sample event checklist in this book.

The third checklist pertains to 'Making Travel Arrangements,' and I've also included a sample for this in the book.

Lastly, I'd like to highlight the 'End of Calendar Year for October' Checklist. This checklist holds particular importance as it lays the groundwork for the upcoming year. In October, I initiate the process of sending out annual invites for various events, such as one-on-one meetings, quarterly meetings, and board meetings, ensuring a smooth transition into the new year.

Event Checklist

If you've been tasked with organizing an event for your company and are unsure where to begin or need a step-by-step checklist to guide you, you're in the right place. Here's a comprehensive checklist I've created to help you through the process:

Initial Meeting with Requestor:
Sit down with the person requesting the event and ask these key questions:
- What is the event's primary objective? (e.g., client appreciation dinner)

- How many guests are expected, including staff? How many staff members will be invited?
- What date is the event being held.
- Is entertainment or guest speakers required? If so, specify the type.
- What is the allocated budget for the event? Is it all-inclusive (covering catering, venue, décor, entertainment/speaker), or are separate budgets allocated for specific elements?
- Determine the preferred venue location.
- Discuss any potential theme.
- Decide if table place cards are needed.
- Determine whether name tags are required.
- Explore options for table centrepieces; common choices include flowers or balloons.

Venue Selection:
- Create a list of potential venues and contact them to inquire about pricing and availability.
- Be aware of venues that may charge separately for venue hire and catering, or those with a minimum spend requirement.
- Visit the selected venue(s) to assess if they meet your needs and check reviews from previous events.

Budget Assessment:
- Based on your budget and preferences, finalize your choice for venue, catering, drinks package, and entertainment/speaker (if needed).
- Compile a list of potential entertainment/speaker options and obtain cost estimates. Ensure you review their credentials and read reviews before making a decision.

Obtain the list of invitees and add them to a spreadsheet (if not already done). Prepare a standby list of potential clients to invite if any declines are received from the original list.

Create the Event Invitation:
- Draft the invitation with the following details:
  - Company name.

- Event title.
- Date and time.
- Venue name and address.
- Dress code or theme (if applicable).
- RSVP date.
- RSVP email address.
- Inquire about dietary requirements.

If the invitation is sent at least ten weeks before the event, set the RSVP date for six weeks prior. This allows for inviting other clients if initial invitees decline.

Establish a dedicated email address for sending invites and receiving RSVPs. Alternatively, set up a dedicated email folder to avoid losing RSVPs in your inbox.

Dietary Requirements:
- Maintain a list of dietary requirements, and for seated meals, assign table numbers next to names for catering purposes.
- Ensure that catering for cocktail parties includes options for various dietary needs (e.g., gluten-free, vegan/vegetarian) to accommodate all guests.

Managing RSVPs:
- Upon receiving an RSVP, record it in the spreadsheet alongside the guest's name.
- If a guest declines, consider inviting someone from the standby list, adjusting the RSVP date as necessary.
- One day after the RSVP deadline, review the spreadsheet and follow up with anyone who hasn't responded.

Preparing for the Event:
Four weeks prior to the event, ensure the following are in order:
- Confirm attendance numbers with the venue and caterers.
- Share the list of dietary requirements with venue/caterers.
- Order flower or balloon arrangements.
- Complete contracts with entertainment/speakers.
- Lock in staff roles for the event.

- Finalize table arrangements, assigning guests to tables.

One Week Before the Event:
Conduct a comprehensive event run-down with:
- Venue manager.
- Caterers.
- Staff to review their roles and event logistics.

Day of the Event:
- Assemble a small event toolkit with essentials like scissors, sticky tape, pens, paper, safety pins, and Velcro tape.
- Place name cards on tables, referencing the table arrangement list.
- Organize name tags in alphabetical order on a check-in table for guests.
- Bring at least four copies of the attendee list to hand out to staff, for fast and efficient guest check-in.
- Arrive at the venue at least two hours early, accompanied by at least one staff member to assist with preparations.
- Ensure other staff members arrive at least an hour before the event.
- After guests arrive and find their seats, engage with them while maintaining professionalism.

By adhering to this comprehensive checklist, you'll be well-equipped to manage all aspects of your company event effectively and ensure a successful and memorable experience for all attendees.

Travel Checklist

When coordinating my executive's travel plans, particularly for international trips, precision is paramount. The last thing I want is for them to:

- Miss a flight.
- Become stranded at an unfamiliar airport due to oversight on visas or transportation.
- Incorrectly schedule meetings because of time zone discrepancies.

Personally, I tend to be rather meticulous when arranging travel, as I'm naturally anxious about these possibilities. In fact, I vividly recall a situation early in my career at a company where my executive was a frequent traveller. On his initial trip, I regrettably failed to factor in the time zone difference, resulting in me adding an incorrect meeting time to my executive's Outlook calendar. Consequently, he missed the meeting, leading to understandable dissatisfaction. While mistakes are inevitable, the objective is to minimize them and never repeat the same error twice.

I'd like to share my travel checklist, which I've devised to prevent potential travel mishaps. I'll simplify it as much as possible, bearing in mind that it can be tailored to your specific needs.

Imagine my executive needs to travel from Sydney to Melbourne, then to Perth, followed by Darwin, and finally back to Sydney. They provide me with the dates and approximate departure times. During the booking process, I may notice that some of the desired flight times aren't available due to remote airport locations with limited daily flights. In such cases, I make a note explaining my choices and communicate this to my executive.

Once all bookings are complete, I enter the details into the table below. This table serves as a comprehensive record of booked flights and accommodations, with space for cost tracking if needed.

The Executive Assistant Toolkit

Travel Checklist

Name of traveller: _____

Dest: _____ Date: _____ Approx time: _____ | Dest: _____ Date: _____ Approx time: _____

Dest: _____ Date: _____ Approx time: _____ | Dest: _____ Date: _____ Approx time: _____

Dest: _____ Date: _____ Approx time: _____ | Dest: _____ Date: _____ Approx time: _____

Travel information

Day & Date	Departure Time	Arrival Local Time	Destination	Cost of flight	Flight #	Hotel Name and address	Check in date	Check out date	Cost of accom.	Visa required Y/N
Mon 15 Jun	08:15am	09:20am	Melbourne	$437	QF345	Grand Hyatt	15 June	17 Jun	$850	No

International Travel

☐ Is there a visa required? **Yes/No**

If yes, which ones?

....

(Check the Government Website: Begin by researching whether a visa is necessary for the destination. If a visa is required, check if it can be obtained upon arrival at the destination airport or if it necessitates sending the passport to the destination's embassy in your country before departure. Additionally, determine the processing time for obtaining the visa and the associated costs. If the departure date is scheduled before the visa can be issued, investigate the possibility of expediting the visa process. If expedited processing isn't available, consider advising your executive to postpone their departure until the visa is obtained).

    ☐ Applied and waiting for approval.
    ☐ Visa received.
    ☐ Visa issued at destination upon arrival.
    ☐ Visa not required.

☐ Is local currency required before travel? **Yes/No**
    ☐ Currency arranged.

☐ Time zones have been noted and entered into executive's Outlook?

- ☐ Researched the following location information and added to itinerary notes, such as:
    - ☐ Risks, i.e., pickpockets, etc.
    - ☐ Customs, tipping etiquette.
    - ☐ What the weather is going to be like around the time of the executive's trip.
    - ☐ Places to see in free time.
- ☐ Phone
    - ☐ International roaming turned on.
    - ☐ International roaming not needed.
    - ☐ SIM card to be purchased at destination airport.
- ☐ Is travel insurance required? **Yes/No**
    - ☐ Arranged.
- ☐ Are all time zones accounted for in calendar and itinerary? **Yes/No**

All-Travel Section
This section should be completed for all travel:
- ☐ All flights booked.
- ☐ E-tickets received.
- ☐ Frequent flyer number added to booking.
- ☐ Time of departure and time of arrival to destination added to the executive's Outlook calendar with e-ticket attachments. (*remember time zones*)
- ☐ Accommodation booked.
- ☐ Reward number added to accommodation booking.
- ☐ Added the time of check-in (*remembering time zones*), along with hotel name, address, and phone number to executive's Outlook calendar with confirmation attached.
- ☐ Downloaded all apps required for destination.
- ☐ Ground travel pre-booked, i.e., driver / hire car / taxi /courtesy car / train / shuttle bus; details added to the executive's Outlook with confirmations.

☐ Created and printed itinerary for the executive with all documentation, confirmations, and e-tickets the executive will require for their trip.

With this checklist, simply mark off each item as you complete it, ensuring that all relevant details are added to your executive's Outlook calendar, including attachments, and considering all time zones.

The final task on this list is to generate and print your executive's itinerary, including all necessary documents, confirmations, and e-tickets required for the trip. Remember, there's no universal checklist – tailor it to suit both your needs and those of your executive.

End of Calendar Year Checklist to Complete in October

Use this checklist to help get on top of tasks for the following year. This is my checklist.

October
☐ Add public holidays into the following year's calendar if Outlook hasn't automatically updated the calendar.
☐ Create a spreadsheet of all dates for the following year for the following meetings, to discuss with the CEO.
  ☐ board meeting – quarterly
  ☐ risk committee meeting – quarterly
  ☐ town hall meeting - quarterly
☐ Once approval is given by the CEO for the above meetings, send out Outlook invites.
☐ Board meeting invite sent to Board members.
☐ Risk Committee invite sent to Risk Committee members.
☐ Town hall meeting invite sent to all staff.

- ☐ Send out recurring invites for the following year for the leadership teams one-on-one meetings.
- ☐ Send out invites to the leadership team for their half-yearly performance review in January.
- ☐ Send out invites for all the quarterly client meetings for the following year.
- ☐ End of May, send individual invites to all the leadership team to go over their budget for the following financial year in July.
- ☐ Go through next year's Outlook calendar and make sure no meeting invites fall on a public holiday or conflict with other meetings, and if so, change to a more suitable date.
- ☐ Discuss with the CEO when he would like to have the leadership team offsites.
- ☐ Send out tentative leadership offsite invites to the leadership team.
- ☐ Prepare some Christmas e-cards for the CEO, then add them to their Outlook for the first week in November so they can choose which one they would like sent out to clients.
- ☐ Add a prompt in the CEO's calendar the third week of November to draft a Christmas message, one to clients and another to staff.

November
- ☐ Follow up with the CEO to see if the Christmas messages have been written.
  - ☐ Staff message completed.
  - ☐ Client message completed.
- ☐ Follow up with the CEO to see if the Christmas e-cards have been chosen.
  - ☐ Staff e-card chosen.
  - ☐ Client e-card chosen.
- ☐ Call the venue you have booked for your Christmas party and confirm your booking that you made back in August.

December

- ☐ In the first week of December, distribute an email to all staff members inquiring if they wish to participate in a Kris Kringle / White Elephant gift exchange during the staff Christmas party. Additionally, include the maximum spending limit for the gifts in the email.
- ☐ Compile the names of all participants in the Kris Kringle / White Elephant gift exchange and place each name in a container, such as a hat. Encourage everyone to draw a name from the hat.
- ☐ All names have been drawn from the hat, and each person now knows the name of the individual for whom they will be purchasing a Kris Kringle / White Elephant gift.
- ☐ Send the CEO Christmas e-card message to the client by the second week of December.
- ☐ Send the Christmas e-card message to staff before the 20th December or before the CEO goes on vacation.
- ☐ Make a list of the leadership team's Christmas vacation and who they have delegated their authority to whilst they are on leave.
- ☐ Email the above leave and delegate list to everyone on the leadership team.
- ☐ All boxes in this checklist have been ticked.

How to Create a Work Newsletter and Some Topic Ideas

Crafting a company newsletter can be a gratifying endeavour, but the process of creating, publishing, and distributing it can be quite demanding, especially when you rely on information from various sources.

Having created numerous company newsletters over the years, I've accumulated valuable insights to share from this experience.

If you're starting from scratch and searching for a template, I highly recommend Canva, which offers a variety of free newsletter templates. You can also customize them with your company's colours, logo, or letterhead as needed. Alternatively, you can explore the internet for "newsletter templates" to gather ideas on structuring and formatting your newsletter.

The next crucial step is determining the content of your company newsletter. With a multitude of options available, I've outlined some suggestions below. Ultimately, the content and tone can be tailored to your company's preferences, whether you opt for a formal or casual approach.

- Departmental updates
  - CEO update (this would always come first)
  - HR
    - internal/external job postings
    - payday information
    - performance review dates
    - anniversaries
    - birthdays (*make sure you have the consent from the person you want to include in the newsletter*).
    - who's on leave
    - promotions
    - resignations
    - new hires
  - Marketing
    - product news and updates
    - upcoming sponsorships
    - upcoming events
    - snapshot of past events
  - Information Technology
    - new software releases
    - software updates
    - downtime for upgrades
  - Risk & Compliance
    - regulatory updates
    - policy updates

- 'Did You Know?' sections: This is a great gap filler between sections; they can be placed on a corner of each or some pages.
- Highlight a member of staff: I call this section 'Ten Questions with (and the name of the person).' I will outline the ten questions I ask the person further down in this section.
- Tips on how to stay healthy
- Book club
- Recommendations such as TV shows or books
- 'Brain Teaser' competition and the winner gets a voucher.
- What's happening in your town or city? (This one might not be for companies that have branches in different states or countries because there would be too much to list.)

As you can see, there is a multitude of options to consider when adding content to your newsletter, and you might even have your own unique ideas.

Here is the set of information and questions I typically send to the staff member I'm featuring in the "Ten Questions With" section of the newsletter. Feel free to customize these questions to align with your company's style and culture, and most importantly, enjoy the process.

About me:
Please supply a brief paragraph or two about the following:
- *Any siblings / partner / kids/ animals. Where were you born, where did you grow up, and any titbits about you that you would like to add.*
- *Attach minimum two, maximum four photos that relate to the 'about me' information.*

Answer the following questions:
1. *If you could be famous for anything, what would you be famous for?*
2. *If you could have a superpower, what would it be and why?*

3. If you had to create a bucket list, what would be number one on that list?
4. If you could spend time with anyone from history, who would it be and why?
5. Should pineapple go on pizza?
6. What would be the first thing you'd do if you won $1,000,000 in the lottery?
7. What's one piece of advice you would give your younger self?
8. What's your favourite way to spend a day off?
9. If you were handed a plane ticket right now to anywhere in the world, where would you go?
10. What's your dream car?

Take your time with your newsletter; refining the layout and content may require several iterations to align with your company's needs. Experiment with different formats each month until you find the one that best fits your organization. Don't forget to seek feedback from your executive.

I'm in the early stages of developing an animated newsletter using Canva to boost staff engagement. There isn't much to share about it at the moment, but once I have something together, I will share it on my YouTube channel.

PART EIGHT

Tell Me More!

Tasks You Should Do... and Not Your Executive

A fundamental pillar of the executive assistant role is the efficient management of your executive's time. Time is their most precious resource, and all our efforts should be dedicated to safeguarding and optimizing it. I'd like to highlight key areas where you can effectively save your executive's valuable time.

Here are just a few suggestions.

Communications: Assistants are responsible for drafting most communications to staff on behalf of the executive. This includes meeting notes, updates, or news. They should also manage inbound communications, ensuring only necessary items reach the executive.

Research: Assistants conduct research on behalf of their executive, ranging from gathering information about new clients and their businesses to reviewing annual reports of other organizations or researching business contacts on platforms like LinkedIn.

Administration of Documents: Assistants oversee the administration of records for the executive. They decide which documents the executive should review and forward relevant documents to other staff members or schedule them for future reference. Assistants also coordinate time in the executive's schedule for paperwork and reading.

Email and Diary Management: Assistants handle all aspects of email management, including responding to incoming emails and sending emails on behalf of the executive. They have complete control over the executive's calendar, and the executive should direct all meeting requests to the assistant. Changes to the diary are discussed during daily catch-up meetings.

Business Travel: Assistants manage all aspects of the executive's business travel, both domestic and international.

They discuss updates and travel plans with the executive during daily catch-up meetings.

Purchase Orders, Invoices, and Expenses: Assistants oversee financial matters related to the executive, including handling purchase orders, invoices, and expenses. They may have the authority to sign off on invoices and expenses for the executive's direct reports or schedule time in the executive's calendar for signing documents.

Holiday and Sick Leave Records: When the executive manages a department, assistants handle all holiday and sick leave records. They may have the authority to approve standard holiday requests and short-term sick leave.

Administrative Systems: Assistants take control of all administrative systems and day-to-day office management tasks. This includes maintaining office equipment, ordering stationery, managing office furniture, and booking and maintaining meeting rooms. The assistant ensures the smooth operation of office administration, allowing the executive to focus on larger matters.

Suppliers: Assistants are responsible for managing suppliers. This involves researching new suppliers, maintaining contracts, handling communications, and managing invoices.

Point of Contact: Assistants act as the primary point of contact for matters related to their executive. They filter communications, meeting requests, administrative tasks, and financial matters, saving the executive time for strategic priorities.

What Makes an Executive Assistant a Superstar

Becoming a superstar executive assistant isn't a path everyone chooses. It requires embracing teachable moments, constant practice, and an unwavering commitment to continuous learning. It's not merely about fulfilling your job duties; it's about elevating your role beyond its initial scope and becoming a vital asset to your organization or department. To achieve this, you must possess an in-depth understanding of the business or department you serve.

However, it's important to acknowledge that your effectiveness as an executive assistant can sometimes be influenced by your executive's management style. Some executives tend to micromanage, making it challenging to showcase your capabilities. Others may require time to build trust in your abilities, resulting in a gradual process. There are also those executives who may not readily recognize the value you bring, regardless of your efforts to improve their work life.

In certain cases, no matter how much you enhance their daily operations and go above and beyond, some executives might take your contributions for granted. They may expect exceptional support as the norm, making it difficult for them to fully appreciate your superstar qualities. Remember, this doesn't diminish your capabilities; sometimes, your true worth shines through despite such circumstances.

Here are some exemplary qualities of a superstar executive assistant:

Proactive Task Completion: They anticipate their executive's needs and initiate tasks before being asked. For instance, if a client emails requesting a meeting, the assistant schedules it promptly, sparing their executive the effort.

Initiative: Superstar assistants identify opportunities to contribute more effectively. If they see their executive working on a task they can handle, they offer to take over, freeing up their executive's time.

Resourcefulness: They are resourceful problem solvers. When faced with unfamiliar tasks or topics, they proactively research using online resources like Google or YouTube to quickly gain knowledge.

Continuous Learning: A commitment to ongoing learning is a hallmark of a superstar assistant. They understand that knowledge is limitless and actively seek opportunities to expand their skills and expertise.

Proactive Process Improvement: They identify areas where processes can be optimized and take the initiative to document and implement improvements. They don't wait for someone else to do it.

Effective Negotiation: Superstar assistants are not afraid to negotiate, whether it's haggling for stationery prices or other regular purchases. Their negotiation skills contribute to cost savings for the company.

Business Acumen: They invest time in understanding their organization's business thoroughly, which enhances their business acumen and decision-making abilities.

Trusted Extension: Over time, they become a trusted extension of their executive, capable of making decisions when needed, particularly in non-legal or non-financial matters. This trust is built through consistent reliability and understanding the business.

I once worked for a CEO who encouraged me to take decisive actions rather than delay, even if there was a chance of making a mistake. His belief was that it's easier to seek forgiveness afterward than to seek permission beforehand.

Building this level of trust with an executive is a gradual process, and acquiring in-depth knowledge about the business significantly contributes to earning that trust.

Diverse Knowledge: They cultivate a broad range of knowledge. They read, engage in learning, and gain real-world experiences, enabling them to converse effectively with colleagues, clients, and people from various backgrounds and levels.

Exceptional Project Delivery: When assigned a project, they not only complete it on time but go the extra mile, adding thoughtfulness and creativity to their work.

Confidence: Superstar assistants are confident in their abilities. They acknowledge that mistakes happen but learn from them to improve, avoiding the repetition of the same errors.

In summary, a superstar executive assistant is a proactive, resourceful, and continuously learning professional who adds value to their role by going beyond expectations, fostering trust, and maintaining confidence in their abilities. They are indispensable assets to their executives and organizations.

What is an Inefficient Executive Assistant?

Now, let's shift our focus to the opposite end of the spectrum - the inefficient executive assistant. During my career, I've encountered numerous executive assistants who believed they were performing well when, in fact, their performance left much to be desired.

What made this situation more challenging was their resistance to self-improvement. Instead of seeking ways to enhance their skills, they engaged in negative talk about their colleagues, attempting to elevate themselves by degrading others. It seemed that they were more interested in the prestige associated with the executive assistant role than in excelling at it.

To be clear, lacking certain skills doesn't prevent you from becoming an effective executive assistant. However, it necessitates a willingness to address these deficiencies and actively work on improving them.

Here are some traits and behaviours that can characterize an inefficient executive assistant:

- Unwillingness to improve existing skills or acquire new ones.
- Overreliance on memory without taking notes, resulting in tasks being forgotten and left undone.
- Maintaining "to-do" lists but failing to reference them, causing tasks to slip through the cracks.
- Engaging in gossip about colleagues, which is unprofessional and compromises neutrality.
- Breaching confidentiality by sharing sensitive information with co-workers, demonstrating an inability to keep secrets.
- Failing to research and problem-solve independently, instead repeatedly seeking guidance from their executive for task completion.
- Focusing on their daily routine without proactively inquiring about how they can assist their executive more effectively.
- Limited proficiency with software tools like Microsoft Suite or Google Suite, coupled with a reluctance to expand their knowledge.
- An unwillingness to learn from mistakes, often attributing blame to others or making excuses rather than taking corrective action.

- Poor attention to detail, displaying a lack of commitment to ensuring accuracy.
- Constantly needing explicit instructions and supervision, rather than demonstrating the ability to work autonomously.
- Discomfort with the dynamic nature of their role and difficulty in handling challenges.
- Unapproachable demeanour and a lack of emotional intelligence, despite the expectation that executive assistants should be open, perceptive, and the organization's eyes and ears.

The Case of the Sabotaging Executive Assistant

"Coming together is a beginning.
Keeping together is progress.
Working together is success."
Henry Ford

Throughout my extensive experience as an executive assistant, I've observed a tendency among some of my peers: to compete rather than collaborate. While there are exceptions, this issue occurs more often than it should.

In larger organizations, I've encountered executive assistants who withhold valuable information or resources that could assist their colleagues. Let me share a specific incident that illustrates this point. When I started at a multinational corporation, I was tasked with supporting two executives handling departments across various countries. There were no handover notes or clear guidance. As I struggled to navigate the complexities of the role and identify which executive assistants supported the relevant executives, a colleague nearby revealed that she maintained a detailed spreadsheet listing executives and their respective assistants.

I kindly asked if she could share this resource with me, to which she agreed. However, she never followed through with sending it, I asked again and yet I never received it, I also realised that she had changed her mind in regard to sharing the document. I understood that it might have been an effort to compile and maintain this information, and she might have faced similar challenges when she began her role. Nevertheless, I would have gladly shared my own knowledge in return because I believe in the collective success of executive assistants.

Another instance occurred when I temporarily worked at a legal firm in Hong Kong. I was supporting one of the partners, and, once again, there were no handover notes to guide me. I turned to two executive assistants seated nearby for assistance with my inquiries. Regrettably, their responses were curt and unhelpful, often a simple "I don't know" or "I'm too busy to help you." This approach cultivated an environment of competition rather than collaboration.

The drive to compete often stems from a desire to appear superior to other executive assistants in the organization. However, what we should recognize is that every executive has unique needs, and the crucial factor is being the right executive assistant for your executive. Compatibility in terms of skills, personality, and comfort with each other is essential.

We should prioritize sharing our knowledge and experiences with one another. Imagine if the executive assistant I had approached had shared the spreadsheet I requested, and, in return, I provided her with my own manual. Such collaboration could have made us both better executive assistants. Our strength lies in empowering one another.

Whenever you have the chance to assist a fellow executive assistant, embrace it. You may discover that the rewards extend beyond your expectations. Strive to be the executive assistant who genuinely wishes success for others in the field.

The Executive Assistant with ADHD Tendencies – Tips to Help Keep You Focused

Many assistants often feel reluctant to reveal their vulnerabilities out of fear of being judged. They tend to present themselves in the best possible light, fearing that others might perceive them as incompetent. Today, I want to break that barrier and discuss something that used to make me feel vulnerable. My hope is that by sharing my experiences, I can help others facing similar challenges in their roles as executive assistants.

ADHD was not a topic of discussion while I was growing up or when I began my career. In fact, I had never even heard of it. Before I proceed, I want to clarify that I have not been formally diagnosed with ADHD. After all these years, I remain uncertain whether I want an official diagnosis. However, I do experience some symptoms associated with ADHD.

So, what is ADHD?
This is the definition according to ADDitudemag.com:
ADHD (attention deficit hyperactivity disorder) is the term commonly used to describe a neurological condition with symptoms of inattention, distractibility, and poor working memory. ADHD symptoms in adults include trouble focusing on work, habitually forgetting appointments, easily losing track of time, and struggling with executive functions.

My school years were not without their challenges. Although I managed to pass all my subjects, it was far from easy. It wasn't a matter of lacking intelligence; rather, I realized that I had a unique way of learning that didn't align with the standard teaching methods employed in schools. Unfortunately, this understanding didn't come to me during my schooling years, as theconcept of different learning styles wasn't a prominent part of early education.

I would highly recommend that if you're unsure about your learning style, take some time to research and discover what works best for you. In my case, I eventually learned that I excelled when I was shown how to do something, rather than simply being told.

When I embarked on my journey as an executive assistant thirty years ago, I faced challenges related to my soft skills. However, I didn't have readily available resources like Google to search for solutions. Instead, I had to rely on trial and error, experimenting with different approaches to improve my efficiency and effectiveness in the role.

I want to share some of the things that held me back from becoming a great executive assistant for the first few years of stepping into that role. I want to also share what I have done about rectifying and assisting me with those issues.

Here are some of my problem areas and the tools I have implemented to help work around those problems. Earlier in this book, I mentioned in detail, some of the helpful techniques I will be mentioning below.

Forgetfulness: Forgetfulness used to be a significant challenge for me. After meetings with my executive, I would often walk back to my desk and promptly forget the details of our conversation. To counter this, I developed a technique using my notebook, different coloured pens, and a highlighter. I began taking detailed notes during our discussions, ensuring that I captured all relevant information. This way, even if I couldn't immediately attend to the tasks, I had a clear record to refer back to at any time.

For external clients I rarely communicated with, I faced a similar memory challenge, struggling to recall important details like their executive assistant's name, company affiliation, and position. To address this, I created a list in my executive assistant manual, systematically recording these essential details for easy reference.

Learning new software: Learning new software was another hurdle for me. To navigate this, I started documenting the step-by-step procedures as I learned, including screenshots for clarity. I then reviewed and refined these instructions using my notes and added them to my executive assistant manual for future referral.

Stumbling over words: Stumbling over words during conversations was a result of my mind racing ahead to the next thought. I found it challenging to remain present and articulate my thoughts smoothly. To overcome this, I practiced staying in the present moment, consciously focusing on the ongoing conversation. While it wasn't easy and required ongoing effort, this practice significantly improved my communication.

Attention to detail: Early in my career, during my mid-twenties, I struggled significantly with attention to detail. I was often so focused on completing tasks that I overlooked the importance of thoroughly checking for errors. This behaviour persisted for a while, but without any major repercussions, until one fateful day when a significant error occurred.

I had scheduled an important meeting in a different state, but unfortunately, I failed to account for the correct time zone. As a result, my executive missed the meeting, and his frustration was palpable. In fact, he expressed his displeasure quite vocally; his words were sharp and direct.

This incident served as a powerful wake-up call for me. I realized the gravity of my oversight and the impact it could have on my executive and the organization as a whole. It was a turning point in my career. From that day forward, I was determined to improve my attention to detail significantly, vowing to never allow such a mistake to happen again.

I have become exceptionally vigilant in my work practices. Before finalizing any task, I meticulously review it at least twice. When handling flight arrangements, I am particularly thorough. I painstakingly verify the dates and times, conducting multiple checks before confirming the booking.

Furthermore, when adding flight details to my executive's calendar, I am extra cautious about inputting the correct time zones into his Outlook. Additionally, I ensure that all associated meetings are scheduled in the appropriate time zone to eliminate any potential scheduling discrepancies.

I thrive in the morning, making it my ideal time to tackle tasks requiring meticulous attention to detail. To ensure I have a quiet environment for handling critical assignments, I prioritize working in a tranquil space.

Moreover, I have implemented a proactive approach to avoid repeating past mistakes. Whenever an error occurs, I promptly establish new systems and safeguards to prevent its recurrence. This commitment to continuous improvement ensures that my performance remains consistently high.

Procrastination: Dealing with procrastination was another challenge. I used to delay tasks, especially those I found boring, until the last minute. However, I adopted the time-blocking method, scheduling specific slots in my calendar to complete tasks, and disciplined myself to stick to these blocks. This approach proved effective in overcoming procrastination and ensuring timely task completion.

Emails: I developed a strategy for handling complex or convoluted emails. Instead of grappling with wordy or disorganized messages, I summarized them using bullet points and then sent the summarized version back to the sender for confirmation. This helped clarify their requests, often eliminating the need for further clarification.

These techniques and strategies have been instrumental in overcoming my personal challenges and enhancing my effectiveness as an executive assistant. Numerous resources are readily available to help in overcoming personal challenges.

Rita Gunning

Unlike my early days in this role when such support was scarce, you now have access to a wealth of tools and guidance.

Don't lose hope if you encounter setbacks; persistence is key. If your initial approach doesn't yield results, keep searching for alternative methods. My own journey involved a considerable amount of trial and error, but it ultimately led me to where I am today. Even after three decades, I continue to learn and adapt, highlighting the importance of ongoing growth and improvement.

The Executive Assistant Toolkit

Rita Gunning

Author Biography

Rita Gunning's journey began in Beirut, Lebanon, before she embarked on a transformative chapter by immigrating to Australia alongside her family when she was just six years old. Cultivating a deep sense of belonging, she proudly identifies as Australian. With a remarkable career spanning three decades, Rita Gunning has established herself as a seasoned Executive Assistant.

Her global explorations have taken her to numerous countries, where she not only visited but also resided in seven diverse nations. This international exposure enriched her professional repertoire as she served as an Executive Assistant across various cultural landscapes, including dynamic environments like Hong Kong and Japan.

Diversifying her endeavours, Rita assumed the role of a silent partner in an Australian real estate enterprise in 2011. Her entrepreneurial spirit further flourished as she founded and managed a Marketing Company, in addition to successfully owning and overseeing a vibrant café/restaurant in Hollywood, Florida. This multifaceted journey has honed Rita's comprehensive understanding of business operations and the intricate facets of an Executive Assistant's role.

Rita Gunning's passion for sharing her wealth of experience led her to establish the Executive Assistant Oasis YouTube channel and a thriving Facebook group. Through these platforms, she imparts her insights, wisdom, and guidance, fostering a community of learning and growth for fellow Executive Assistants and business enthusiasts alike.

www.ingramcontent.com/pod-product-compliance
Lightning Source LLC
Chambersburg PA
CBHW062052290426
44109CB00027B/2800